The Threat of the Lesbian Vampire

Cäcilia Glachs

The Threat of the Lesbian Vampire

in Sheridan Le Fanu's "Carmilla", Whitley Strieber's "The Hunger" and Jewelle Gomez's "The Gilda Stories"

Reihe Geisteswissenschaften

Imprint
Any brand names and product names mentioned in this book are subject to trademark, brand or patent protection and are trademarks or registered trademarks of their respective holders. The use of brand names, product names, common names, trade names, product descriptions etc. even without a particular marking in this work is in no way to be construed to mean that such names may be regarded as unrestricted in respect of trademark and brand protection legislation and could thus be used by anyone.

Cover image: www.ingimage.com

Publisher:
AV Akademikerverlag
is a trademark of
International Book Market Service Ltd., member of OmniScriptum Publishing Group
17 Meldrum Street, Beau Bassin 71504, Mauritius

ISBN: 978-3-639-40417-3

TABLE OF CONTENTS

1. Introduction

> And this vampire thing; what is a vampire?
> Who projected that image onto you?
> My guess is, the people of Transylvania created you
> out of boredom and frustration.
> (Virginia Woolf in *I, Vampire*, 201)

Vampires have haunted the literary, cinematic and theatrical world in various shapes and appearances. Depending on the age, its set of beliefs and moral standards, vampires have symbolised varying desires, traits or anxieties. Therefore, it is difficult to find a definition for the creature we know as 'the vampire' that unifies all its multifarious depictions throughout the years. In his book *The Monster With a Thousand Faces* Brian Frost describes the creature as "a parasitic force or being, malevolent and self-seeking by nature, whose paramount desire is to absorb the life force or ingest the vital fluids of a living organism in order to sate its perverse hunger and perpetuate its unnatural existence" (Frost 27). Despite the negative connotations, vampires have become a source of fascination for human beings, which may largely be due to the eroticism that is connected to the act of bloodsucking. Also, the veil of secrecy that surrounds these beings, the mystery of their existence adds to the appeal of vampires. From the early nineteenth century on, vampires have been seen as dangerous, charismatic and sexual predators. Vampire stories cautioned human beings to beware of the dangers of sex and the loss of one's soul. Thus, vampires have become icons set opposite humanity and its world of order and security. It is the vampires' actions, their behaviour, and the comparison of their way of life to that of humans which allows human beings to define humanity and determine what being human actually involves. What both species seem to have in common is their will to live and, furthermore, their sexual drive. Yet, while the vampires' kiss sends shivers of excitement down the reader's spine, the sexuality of some human beings that did not conform to the norm that has for a long time been heterosexuality, gives shivers of unease to some readers. Queer people, i.e. people who are not heterosexual but either homo-, trans-, or bisexual, have for a long time led lives in some respects similar to that of literary vampires. Like the creatures of the night, queers were confined to secrecy for many centuries. Since their sexuality was considered to be unnatural and a breach of the laws of society, queer people had to live their sexuality in private - behind locked doors, just as vampires are forced to exist hidden and concealed from the human eye. Both were perceived as threats to humanity, the former to morality and social standards, the latter to our lives and souls. A combination of the two, namely queer vampires, and to add to the thrill, female ones, increases the hazard considerably.

In that light, this paper is an examination of the threat that Sheridan Le Fanu's vampire Carmilla poses in his novella of the same name (1872). Furthermore, two novels of the twentieth century, *The Hunger* (1981) by Whitley Strieber and *The Gilda Stories* (1991) by Jewelle Gomez, are examined with respect to the danger that their lesbian vampires represent to their female victims and the societies around them. Thereby, next to the most obvious threat they pose due to their bloody diet, their sexualities play an important part as well and will be analysed in the light of their respective centuries' moral standards based on a historical account of (homo-) sexuality and Queer Studies in general.

Yet, it is not only the female vampires' lesbianism that threatens the lives and minds of those around them but also the very fact that they are women. The nineteenth century had strict views especially on the position of men and women in society. Women who did not adhere to these norms, were perceived as potential threats to male dominance. Two other aspects of the otherness of women studied in this paper are Freud's concept of 'the uncanny' and Kristeva's theory of 'the abject'.

I chose Le Fanu's *Carmilla* because it represents a novel written at the end of the nineteenth century, even before Stoker wrote his well known vampire classic *Dracula* (1872). Although the novella was written by a man, the incidents are narrated from the point of view of the vampire's last victim Laura. The novella is a great example of Victorian writing since it illustrates the body of thought common for that time. The vampire's bloody tracks are explained by natural causes at first. The belief in God is supposed to save the pious people from the vampiric "disease" that spreads the country. Gallant men open their houses to the lady vampire, although reluctantly at first, simply because this is what a man is supposed to do when a damsel is in distress. This situation then leads to the unfolding of dangerous events in *Carmilla*.

The Hunger, like *Carmilla* written by a male author, presents a female parasite of an entirely different species. It follows the millennia long existence of Miriam Blaylock, an attractive woman who seduces men and women alike. The novel centres around her courting a heterosexual scientist, Dr. Sarah Roberts, in the 1980s. Here, scientists attempt to find scientific explanations for Miriam's otherness. Hence, she does not only threaten heterosexual norms but also the laws of biological science. Unlike Carmilla, Miriam's experience allows her to live in the end and to continue her haunt of human beings.

Likewise, the lesbian vampire Gilda in Jewelle Gomez's novel survives in the end. I picked this novel in order to include a vampire who is not only a lesbian but also black, like the author who created her. Her life is depicted from her time as a human girl, and her turn into a vampire in the 1850s, to her existence in the year 2050. According to Nina Auerbach, Gilda and her fellow vampires "present no threat" (186). They may not do so physically, yet, the danger they pose is different from Carmilla's. Their threat is a more abstract but not a less serious one.

2. (Homo-) Sexuality – An Overview

> No government has the right to tell its citizens
> when or whom to love.
> The only queer people are those
> who don't love anybody.
> (Rita Mae Brown, speech, 28 August 1982)

2.1. A History of (Homo-) Sexuality – Part I

Both sexuality and lesbianism are important concepts in the reading of *Carmilla,*
The Hunger and *The Gilda Stories.* In order to understand why Le Fanu's
novella is seen as innovative for his time with regard to a lesbian reading, these
notions must be explained. According to Richard Dyer, it is important to
establish frameworks of understanding in order to make sense of ourselves as
well as of everyone around us. Therefore, people are categorised as well.
These categorisations provide certain sets of codes within which mankind is
enabled to live and operate (see Dyer, *Culture* 1). In the late nineteenth century,
the science of sexuality, sexology, developed. For the first time, it provided a
detailed descriptive system for the classification of sexual types of persons
(heterosexual, homosexual, bisexual and their variants) "and their forms of
sexual desire" (Bristow 13), e.g. sadism, masochism or fetishism. The German
Karl Heinrich Ulrichs (1825 – 1895) also devised a typology of sexual variation
in the second half of the nineteenth century. In it he also investigated
homosexuality, although this was not the term he used in his study. Ulrichs
makes a distinction between those who love the opposite sex and those who
are attracted to the same sex. He called the first group of people Urnings,
named after the god Uranus, and the second group was called Dionings, after
the goddess Dione. Within these two groups he established seven different
sexual types, e.g. Urningings, who in the early twentieth century were named
lesbians (see Bristow 20 ff.). Ulrichs' work paved the way for the modern study
of lesbianism (see Dynes vii). He was criticised, however, for he took the view
that Urnings constitute a third sex with the women containing the soul of men

and vice versa. Bristow claims that this idea persistently influenced twentieth century prejudices against homosexuals like, for instance, the picture of the effeminate gay man and the butch lesbian (see Bristow 21 ff.). Another study that is worth mentioning concerning homosexuality is that of the professor of psychiatry Krafft-Ebing (1840 – 1902), a colleague of Freud's. In his work *Psychopathia Sexualis* (1886) he analyses sexual love from a psychological as well as physiological point of view (see Bristow 26). Furthermore, he also reflects on the legal provision of sexual acts and calls for lawyers to work together with physicians "in all cases of sexual crimes" (Krafft-Ebing 476). Like Ulrichs, Krafft-Ebing calls homosexual persons Urnings, yet, the word homosexual is mentioned in his work as well (see Krafft-Ebing 357). Similarly, he also describes men who feel like women, and vice versa (see Krafft-Ebing 373). It is also interesting to note that in his view "amor lesbicus" (476) has a similar psycho-pathological status as rape, pederasty and bestiality (see Krafft-Ebing 476). He even calls lesbian love "forbidden friendships" (576). In his chapter about "sexual inversion in woman" (390) he explores "this anomaly" (390) and states the following reasons for the fact that homosexuality is less frequent among women than men:

> It is more difficult to gain the confidence of the sexually perverse woman; (2) this anomaly, in so far as it leads to sexual intercourse, *inter feminas*, does not fall (in Germany at any rate) under the criminal code, and therefore remains hidden from public knowledge; (3) sexual inversion does not affect woman in the same manner as it does man, for it does not render woman impotent; (4) because woman (whether sexually inverted or not) is by nature not as sensual and certainly not as aggressive in the pursuit of sexual needs as man, for which reason the inverted sexual intercourse among women is less noticeable, and by outsiders is considered mere friendship. [...]
> (Krafft-Ebing 390)

Like Ulrichs, Krafft-Ebing assigns the traits of *effeminatio* to homosexual men and *viraginity* to homosexual women (see Krafft-Ebing 391). These women, he states, "[assume] definitely the masculine *rôle*" (392). This is due to "[t]he masculine soul [,] heaving in the female bosom" (392). That is why they prefer playing with toys considered to be more appropriate for boys than for girls, like, for instance, soldiers instead of dolls (see Krafft-Ebing 392). The same is true for "manly sports" (392). Krafft-Ebing even goes one step further and presents "[g]ynandry [as] the extreme grade of degenerative homosexuality" (392). The affected women are considered female only because of their genitals, other characteristics that account for being a woman, like action, thought and looks "are those of the man" (392).

It is important to note that sexuality has been studied in various disciplines, such as sexology and psychoanalysis. The French philosopher Michel Foucault wrote three volumes of *The History of Sexuality*, published between 1976 and his death in 1984, which represent innovative reflections on sexuality (see Bristow 168 ff.). In the first volume he published the chapter *The Perverse Implantation* (1976), which, among other things, dealt with homosexuality. According to Foucault, until the nineteenth century sexual practices were governed by three major laws, the civil law, the canonical law and the Christian pastoral. All of these codes dictate what was legitimate and what was not, and they were only concerned with sexual relations within marriage. Later, the discourse focused also on the sexuality of those who the codes of marriage did not apply to (see Foucault 892 ff.). Foucault claims that what followed was a labelling of disparate sexualities. It is important to note that the power exerted in doing so "was not that of interdiction" (Foucault 895), but they involved four operations aiming at more open-mindedness. The second one was concerned with homosexuality. At all times, sodomy had been prohibited, and a person practising that kind of sexual act was a criminal. Johann Heinrich Zedler's *Universal Lexicon* (1731 - 1754), one of the most extensive encyclopedias of eighteenth century Europe, describes sodomy as follows:

> Sodomie [...] bedeutet überhaupt einen jeden unnatürlichen Gebrauch der Zeugungs-Glieder, es sei mit Menschen, oder Vieh. Sie ist dem Gesetze der Natur entgegen. [...] Noch andere mercken an, weil die Sodomiterey nur der Lust halber geschehe; so sei sie dem Gesetze der Natur zuwieder. Man kan beyde Ursachen zusammen nehmen: Den unnatürlichen Gebrauch der Zeugungs-Glieder und die geile Absicht, die man dabey hat; daraus aber auf das deutlichste erkennen, daß ein solcher Beyschlaff wieder den Willen Gottes sey, so fern er auch durch

die Vernunfft aus der Natur des Menschen erkannt wird. [...] so ist
unstreitig die Sodomiterey, oder, wie sie sonst genennet wird, die
stumme Sünde, das schwereste und abscheulichste unter allen
fleischlichen Lastern [...].(Zedler 328)

This means that the perception of heterosexuals and homosexuals differed
widely. Heterosexuals were perceived as individuals who displayed various
traits, one of which was a sexuality they could control. Homosexuals, however,
were characterised solely by their specific sexual desires (see Eder 164). In the
nineteenth century, however, this changed and sodomy was seen as one form
of homosexuality and "the homosexual was now a species" (Foucault 896).
Rather than focusing on the sexual acts and naming them, science
"incorporate[d] [...] [homosexuality] into the individual" (Foucault 896).

2.2. Female Friendship and Sexuality in the Nineteenth Century

From the seventeenth to the nineteenth century romantic friendships between
women were common and socially accepted in England (see Faderman 74). In
the late eighteenth century qualities like "sensibility, faithfulness, and devotion"
(Faderman 75) were valued in women. Yet, intimate contact with men was
forbidden for unmarried women. These friendships allowed young women to
practice romantic feelings with each other and thereby prepared them for
marriage. Social tolerance even condoned elopement of two women, since it
meant that both of them would not lose their good reputation in society. These
friendships were even permitted for married women. Since divorce was no
option for a couple, the woman might be comforted by a female friend, a fact
which did not violate any social rules (see Faderman 75). These women felt
very passionately about each other, swore their love to one another, kissed,
embraced and even vowed to live or die together. They were not, however,
considered to be lesbians (see Faderman 84).

During the nineteenth century the middle class comprised a wide range of professions and income levels. Therefore, it was important to create a unified class identity that would set it apart from the upper and the working class. One way to achieve class coherence was through "shared notions of morality and respectability" (Nead 5). However, not only one single code of respectability existed, definitions of sexuality varied and were often contradictory. There were, for instance, two different standards for male and female sexuality. This is referred to as 'double standard' and means that while "sexual activity in men [was condoned] as a sign of 'masculinity'[,] [...] [it was condemned] [...] in women as a sign of deviant or pathological behaviour" (Nead 6). This means that a woman's respectability in society was dependent on her sexual identity - she was either perceived as a virgin or a whore (see Nead 6). Medical experts had differing opinions on women's respectability. While some claimed that the virtuous woman did not know any sexual desire, others granted women sexual pleasure within the realms of marriage and reproduction (see Nead 19-20). The most valuable aim of a woman was motherhood, it was her "main reason for being and her chief source of pleasure" (Nead 26). It is not surprising that maternal love was considered to be the epitome of feminine purity (see Nead 26).

This notion entails that a sexual relationship between women was unthinkable, although it did exist (see Ledger 126). The nineteenth century also produced two different gender identities: the ideal nineteenth century woman was associated with the private sphere: she stayed at home, kept the house and tended her children. The men, on the other hand, were connected to the public sphere: the worlds of politics and business (see Nead 32). This can be seen in the Victorian metaphor likening men to oaks and women to ivy. In order to grow, the ivy needs the help of the tree, likewise the wife depends on her husband. When the tree is weakened, it may be held up by the ivy, just as a woman may support her husband when he is in trouble (see Nead 17). Thus, women were dependent on men. They were considered to be delicate, weak, and therefore, perpetually sick, yet at the same time morally sound. The perception of the woman during the nineteenth century is important in the reading of *Carmilla* and *The Gilda Stories*. The vampires' sexuality as well as their moral conduct play a significant part in the novels and will be analysed in more detail in chapters 4 and 5.

2.3. A History of (Homo-) Sexuality – Part II

By the end of the nineteenth century, homosexuality had become a topic discussed publicly. Apart from psychologists and physicians also politicians had to deal with it (see Eder 193). After World War I, same-sex acts were still prosecuted. Yet, freedom of opinion, press and assembly led to a boom in homosexual films, magazines and organisations. The sexual and health policy of the National Socialists was strictly against any form of same-sex desire among men. In their point of view, potency was wasted and therefore the expansion of the people threatened. Homosexuality was widely seen as an infectious social disease (see Eder 194-5, see Oosterhuis 392). Furthermore, homosexual men were considered to be dangerous since, in Hitler's view, they effectively organised in secret in order to seize power (see Oosterhuis 392). According to Oosterhuis, of the 50,000 men who had been convicted because of their homosexuality, 'only' between 5,000 and 15,000 were deported to concentration camps (389; see Eder 195). Interestingly, homosexual acts between women still remained unpunished. The ideology of the National Socialists saw women as sexually dependent on men. Hence, lesbian relationships were seen as insignificant and were not considered to be of any danger to the Volksgemeinschaft (see Eder 195). After World War II, sexuality was declared the epitome of everything private (see Eder 212). Homosexual acts were severely punished. During the early 1950s, the sexual morals of the conservative Christian parties were the prevailing ones. Again, homosexual contacts were sanctioned and stigmatised (see Eder 217 ff.).

The 1960s and 1970s are considered the years of sexual liberation (see Eder 224). It was not so much a radical transition but rather a long-term process, and it can be seen as an expression of a conflict between generations. Many young adults were inspired to talk about sexuality that their parents had been cagey about before. Sexuality was discussed publicly and the media saw an unprecedented sex boom. The Kinsey reports, which had first been published in 1948, studied human sexual behaviour based on statistics. When the reports were popularised in the 1960s, it became evident that there was a discrepancy between moral ideals and sexual practices (see Eder 225). Acts which had until then been regarded as abnormal and perverse, were now part of normal sexual life (see Eder 226). Consequently, the law governing sexual offences was liberalised and homosexuals also benefited from that. In Germany, the total ban of same-sex actions among men was lifted in 1969. Austria did so only two years later (see Eder 229). As a consequence, the self-image of gay and lesbian people changed during the 1970s and 1980s. Same-sex desire was still considered to be a central part of the self-perception and perception by others, yet it was not the defining characteristic of homosexuals (see Eder 230-1). It is important to note that there is a difference between homosexual identity and homosexual behaviour. Jagose claims that while the first develops under certain conditions, the latter is omipresent (see Jagose 15). This can also be seen in the following statement by Jeffrey Weeks (see Jagose 15):

> Homosexuality has existed throughout history, in all types of society, among all social classes and peoples, and it has survived qualified approval, indifference and the most vicious persecution. But what have varied enormously are the ways in which various societies have regarded homosexuality, the meanings they have attached to it, and how those who were engaged in homosexual activity viewed themselves. (qtd. in Jagose 15)

2.4. The Formation of Homophile Movements

At the end of the nineteenth century, homophile organisations sought to declare homosexuality a natural human aspect. In 1869, for instance, the Swiss physician Karoly Maria Benkert, who coined the word 'homosexuality' (see Jagose 72), addressed an open letter against a new legislation criminalising homosexual acts to the minister of justice. In this letter he reasoned that "because homosexuality is innate, it can be subject only to the laws of nature, not penal law" (Jagose 23). In 1897 the Scientific Humanitarian Committee was founded by the German neurologist Magnus Hirschfeld. He further developed Karl Ulrichs' thesis of homosexuality as a third sex. The Committee laid emphasis on the innocuousness of homosexuality (see Jagose 23). The Community of the Special was another organisation founded five years later by Benedict Friedländer. It spoke out against the definition of homosexuality "as a biological disposition" (Jagose 23.). Edward Carpenter and Havelock Ellis founded another organisation, the British Society for the Study of Sex Psychology. Unlike the German's, the British society did not focus on changing the penal laws concerning homosexuality but to educate about it. In the 1950s, there were two homophile organisations in America, the Mattachine Society and The Daughters of Bilitis. The Mattachine Society was founded by members of the Communist party whose political aim was "to foster a collective identity among homosexuals" (Jagose 25). The society split up into two groups due to internal conflicts. While the founders considered homosexuals as a social minority, their opponents represented them as "people like everyone else" (Jagose 26). To the latter group, change could only be effected through a cooperation with experts on education, medicine and law. Since the group did not consider gender as an important issue, it discouraged female membership and did not represent lesbians. But The Daughters of Bilitis, an organisation with four lesbian couples as founders, did. They opposed the butch styling of homosexual women and advocated an assimilation of lesbians (see Jagose 26-8). Neither the Mattachine Society nor The Daughters of Bilits managed to become mass movements since it was difficult to establish political organisations in the 1950s as homosexuals. Although these homophile organisations only had limited success, some of their strategies have been adopted by more recent groupings (see Jagose 28-9).

2.5. The Rise of Lesbian Feminism

In the late 1960s and early 1970s the gay and women's movements developed. At first, the feminist movement dissociated itself from lesbianism because it felt lesbianism would be an obstacle in their fight for equal rights for women (see Jagose 45). Nevertheless, heterosexual and homosexual women did organise, for instance in the National Organisation for Women (NOW), the largest and most powerful women's liberation group in the United States. Yet, the homosexuality of the lesbians within NOW and other similar groups, was perceived as a problem. Hence, when the Second Congress to Unite Women was held in May 1970, a group of women, who called themselves 'Lavender Menace', disrupted the congress and presented a paper collectively written by all of them. It discussed "their experience and analysis of discrimination against lesbians in the women's movement" (Jagose 47). Workshops held the next day by members of Lavender Menace brought forth four statements, which were voted to be adopted as resolutions (see Jagose 47):

1. Be it resolved that Women's Liberation is a Lesbian plot.
2. Resolved that whenever the label 'Lesbian' is used against the movement collectively or against women individually, it is to be affirmed, not denied.
3. In all discussions of birth control, homosexuality must be included as a legitimate method of contraception.
4. All sex education curricula must include Lesbianism as a valid, legitimate form of sexual expression and love.
    (Davis 265)

Another paper called 'The Woman-Identified Woman' written by Lavender Menace, who renamed themselves Radicalesbians, was handed out at the congress (see Jagose 47). In it the Radicalesbians defined a lesbian as "the rage of all women condensed to the point of explosion" (Radicalesbians 153). Furthermore, they claim that it is due to male oppression of women that lesbians are discriminated against in society. They orientate towards heterosexual women rather than homosexual men since "lesbianism is also different from male homosexuality, and serves a different function in society"

(Radicalesbians 154). In their view, male domination with reference to lesbianism works as follows:

> Lesbian is the word, the label, the condition that holds women in line. [...] Lesbian is a label invented by the Man to throw at any woman who dares to be his equal, who dares to challenge his prerogatives (including that of all women as part of the exchange medium among men), who dares to assert the primacy of her own needs. (154; see Jagose 48)

They further argue that "in this sexist society, for a woman to be independent means she *can't* be a woman—she must be a dyke" (Jagose 48). According to Jagose, this paper was "both the cause and the effect of lesbian feminist mobilisation in the 1970s" (48).

Another influential article, 'Compulsory Heterosexuality and Lesbian Existence' (1980), was written by Adrienne Rich. Like the Radicalesbians, Rich distances the affiliation of lesbians from homosexual men:

> Lesbians have historically been deprived of a political existence through 'inclusion' as female versions of male homosexuality. To equate lesbian existence with male homosexuality because each is stigmatised is to erase female reality once again. Part of the history of lesbian existence is, obviously, to be found where lesbians, lacking a coherent female community, have shared a kind of social life and common cause with homosexual men. But there are differences: women's lack of economic and cultural privilege relative to men; qualitative differences in female and male relationships [...] In defining and describing lesbian existence I would hope to move toward a dissociation of lesbian from male homosexual values and allegiances. I perceive the lesbian experience as being, like motherhood, a profoundly *female* experience, with particular oppressions, meanings, and potentialities we cannot comprehend as long as we simply bracket it with other sexually stigmatized existences. (649-50; see Jagose 49-50)

Hence, Rich argues for gender, and not sexuality, to be the identificatory factor for lesbians. Her opinion is opposed by Monique Wittig in her essay 'The Straight Mind' (1992). In it she positions lesbianism outside of gender categories: "To destroy 'woman' does not mean that we aim [...] to destroy lesbianism simultaneously with the categories of sex. [...] Lesbian is the only concept I know of which is beyond the categories of sex (woman and man), because the designated subject (lesbian) is *not* a woman, either economically, or politically, or ideologically" (Wittig 20). In Wittig's view the social system of heterosexuality equals male dominance over women. Therefore, lesbians escape the oppression by refusing to submit to the social orders.

2.6   Queer Studies

It is not easy to find a universal definition of 'queer'. The term 'homosexuality' was coined in 1869 (see Jagose 72). Interestingly, the term 'heterosexuality' was only coined eleven years later in 1880 (see Degele 86). Liberationists broke with the first term in the 1960s and started to use the word 'gay'. It was used to counter those sexual categorisations which privileged heterosexuality and considered it to be normal while at the same time regarding homosexuality as an unnatural form of sexuality (see Jagose 72). The shift between these two terms is analysed by Jeffrey Weeks, who explains that they "are not just new labels for old realities: they point to a changing reality, both in the ways a hostile society labelled homosexuality, and in the way those stigmatized saw themselves" (qtd. in Jagose 75). The newest term in the history of words describing same-sex love and desire is 'queer' and it dates back to the early 1990s (see Jagose 76). The etymology of the word already suggests that it has had rather negative connotations in the past. According to *The Oxford dictionary of English etymology*, 'queer' meant "odd, strange" in the sixteenth century (731). In the eighteenth century, it was used to indicate something or someone was "out of sorts, drunk" (731). *The Concise Oxford English Dictionary* gives two definitions of the adjective queer. The first one is "strange; odd" or the rather dated meaning "slightly ill" in British English (1177). The second meaning of the word is the informal and derogatory use of 'queer' for "a homosexual man" (1177). According to Degele, queer is a political collective term for GLBT, an expression describing Gay-Lesbian-Bi- and Transsexuals (see Degele 42). Queer is more inclusive and not as specific as the terms lesbian or gay (see Cooper 18). It does not, however, only comprise non-heterosexual people but also other social outsiders, like women who had opted for an abortion or people with AIDS (see Degele 43). As for the aim of Queer Studies, it is to shed light on what society considers to be normal and, furthermore, what mechanism of exclusion that involves for those who do not fit into the 'normal category' (see Degele 12). Unlike the feminist movements of the 1970s and 1980s, targets for criticism are not the patriarchy and men but beliefs involving gender, sexuality and other normalities, like, for instance, being white. Queer theorists denounce thinking in binary terms (e.g. the model of two sexes), institutions (e.g. marriage) and ideologies (e.g. the male style of leadership) (see Degele 41).

According to Jagose, it was Foucault's work that had a significant impact on lesbian, gay and, consequently, queer scholarship (see Jagose 79 ff.). In his view, sexuality is not so much a natural condition but a discursive production. Furthermore, he does not think of power as a solely repressive force, it is also a productive one (see Jagose 80):

> In defining the effects of power by repression, one accepts a purely juridical conception of that power; one identifies power with a law that says no; it has above all the force of an interdict. Now, I believe that his is a wholly negative, narrow and skeletal conception of power which has been curiously shared. If power was never anything but repressive, if it never did anything but say no, do you really believe that we should manage to obey it? What gives power its hold, what makes it accepted, is quite simply the fact that it does not simply weigh like a force which says no, but that it runs through, and it produces, things, it induces pleasure, it forms knowledge, it produces discourse; it must be considered as a productive network which runs through the entire social body much more than as a negative instance whose function is repression. (see qtd. in Jagose 80)

This means that those sexual identities that have been marginalised are not only oppressed by the power relations but they are also produced by them. Foucault reiterates his opinion in his chapter 'The Perverse Implantation' (1990): "The nineteenth century and our own have been rather the age of multiplication: a dispersion of sexualities, a strengthening of their disparate forms, a multiple implantation of 'perversions.' Our epoch has initiated sexual heterogeneities" (892).

Another book that has been influential for Queer Studies is Judith Butler's *Gender Trouble: Feminism and the Subversion of Identity* (1990), in which she deals with the notion of gender and argues that it is a cultural construct that stipulates heterosexuality. Together with other theorists like Eve Kosofsky Sedgwick, Butler puts emphasis on the fact that Queer Theory is not only concerned with sexuality but also with gender, ethnicity, race and class. Lesbian and gay sexualities, however, remain central to its study (see Cooper 18, 20) Butler writes about "the prohibitions that produce identity along the culturally intelligible grids of an idealized and compulsory heterosexuality. That disciplinary production of gender effects a false stabilization of gender in the interests of the heterosexual construction and regulation of sexuality within the reproductive domain" (118). Furthermore, gender for Butler is "a stylized repetition of acts" (122). This means that she considers gender to be performative. Butler then refigures gender as fiction: "If gender attributes and acts [...] are performative, then there is no preexisting identity by which an act or attribute might be measured; there would be no true or false, real or distorted acts of gender, and the postulation of a true gender identity would be revealed as a regulatory fiction" (122). By opposing the truth of gender, Butler argues for "gender configurations outside the restricting frames of masculinist domination and compulsory heterosexuality" (122). Hence, homosexuality is not naturalised, but gender as a construct that works only in binary systems is questioned.

As for Queer Studies and vampires, Ken Gelder defines "vampire fiction as *essentially* 'queer'" (58). In his chapter about queer vampires he refers not only to *Carmilla*, but also to Byron's *Fragment* (1816). In it, the narrator observes his friend Augustus Darvell. According to Gelder, Darvell's queerness can be seen in the fact that "he ha[s] a power of giving to one passion the appearance of another, in such a manner that it [is] difficult to define the nature of what was working within him" (Byron 2-3; see Gelder 58). Given that the male narrator feels very attracted to Darvell, a queer reading of this description of the character suggests that he is a queer because the narrator himself recognises him as one. Yet, at the same time he is not entirely sure (see Gelder 58-9). Likewise, Polidori's *The Vampyre* (1819) can be read in a queer light. The vampire Lord Ruthven asks Aubrey "to conceal all [he] knows of [Ruthven]" (Polidori 17). And Aubrey swears that "[I]t shall not be known" (17). *It* can either refer to Ruthven's queerness or to him being a vampire. Again, the young man cannot be certain (see Gelder 59).

Richard Dyer discusses the connection between vampirism and homosexuality in his article 'Children of the Night: Vampirism as Homosexuality, Homosexuality as Vampirism' (1988). According to him, vampires have historically been members of the aristocracy. Likewise, homosexuality has been associated by the public with aristocratic writers like Byron or de Sade (see Dyer, *Children* 53). In his view, the vampire has been a symbol for many different things. He "has represented the weight of the past as it lays on the present, or the way the rich live off the poor, or the threat of an unresolved and unpeaceful death [...], or an alternative life-style as it threatens the established order" (54). Yet, the most obvious image of the vampire has been the sexual one (see Dyer, *Children* 54). It has been stated before that in the past, homosexuality had to be lived in secret, otherwise it would have been punished. Similarly, vampires led a secret existence, fearing their mystery to be uncovered (see Dyer, *Children* 59). Also, the vampire is a victim of his own needs, unable to control them, like, for instance, the thirst for blood. Homosexuality was defended in a similar way, namely, that homosexuals cannot help their sexuality (see Dyer, *Children* 61-2). Another similarity between vampirism and homosexuality is that both take place outside of the sanctioned institution of marriage, the only place where up until the 1960s, sex was accepted (see Dyer, *Children* 64).

In 1991, Sue-Ellen Case published her article 'Tracking the Vampire' which links Queer Theory and vampires. According to her, gender is not a defining aspect of Queer Theory. It highlights desire between people of the same sex but it does not signify which sex that is (see Case 382). Case refers to the denaturalisation that queer has experienced throughout history (see Case 383). Being unnatural, "the queer [...] revels in the discourse of the loathsome, the outcast, the idiomatically proscribed position of same-sex desire. [...] The queer is the taboo-breaker, the monstrous, the uncanny" (383). Unsurprisingly, the vampire has often been described in the same way. Another characteristic that vampires share with queers is their inability to procreate naturally. Queer sex has often been dismissed as infertile since people of the same sex cannot, unlike heterosexuals, procreate together. In her study of the representation of lesbians in films, Case uses the vampire, who to her is "the queer in its lesbian mode" (388) as a depiction of transgressive eroticism and sexuality.

3. The Female Vampire

> Actually vampires are as human as anyone;
> In fact, more so.
> (Sterling O'Blivion in *I, Vampire*, 15)

Carol Senf claims that the origin of the literary female vampire can be traced back to myths and folklore (see Senf 200). She refers to Anthony Masters' *The Natural History of the Vampire* (1972), which states that there are various kinds of female vampires (Masters qtd. in Senf 200). Jewish legends, for instance, wrote about Adam's first wife Lilith, who after illicitly uttering God's name transformed into a demon and beguiled young men and killed children. The same is said to be true for Striges and Lamia, the subjects of Roman and Greek legends, who not only murdered children but also drank their blood. So did, according to Malaysian folklore, the female flying demon *Langsuir*. Scottish mythology warns against the *baobham sith* who, transformed into a beautiful woman, takes all of her victims' blood. What most of these creatures have in common is that they can be characterised with at least one of the following three attributes: insubordinate behaviour, blood sucking and overt eroticism (see Senf 200). David Pirie also links vampirism to eroticism and describes the former as follows: "Triumph des Geschlechtlichen über den Tod, des Fleisches über den Geist und der Materie über das Unsichtbare [...]. Er negiert fast alles außer der rein physischen Sinnesbefriedigung. Von allen denkbaren Kosmologien ist er die materialistischste" (Pirie qtd. in Flocke 12). Petra Flocke states that eroticism has always been characterised by taboos and myths, creating an aura that causes anxiety. Likewise, vampirism causes anxiety, since the actions of vampires are unpredictable and the victims are almost always defenceless. The world we live in dictates certain norms and rules, which have to obeyed. Vampires, however, do not adhere to the rules, they give in to their desires (see Flocke 12). Hence, Flocke concludes, vampirism can be seen as "a metaphor for rampant sexuality that transcends boundaries as well as bodies" (Flocke 12, my translation). As for sexuality, the female vampire acts like the male one, she is active and aggressive, although female sexuality is usually associated with passivity. Thus, the female vampire's sexuality has a negative connotation. Unlike a loving and caring mother, the female vampire does not bear her children but bites a person to create a child. The bite then, Flocke continues, is not only a symbol for sexual expressiveness but also for food intake. By sucking her victim's blood, the vampire takes away "Lebenssaft" (13). Flocke compares the extraction of lifeblood to the extraction of sperm, which creates life and therefore essentially is lifeblood[1] (see Flocke 13). The bite itself also is, as Dyer states, often read as a sexual act (see Dyer, *Children* 54-5). Moreover, it is not only the act itself that is reminiscent of sex, it is also the locality where it takes place. Usually that is the privacy of the victim's bedroom, a space that society connects to sex. Similarly, homosexuality has long been a desire that, by law and social constraints, had to take place in private (see Dyer, *Children* 55-57).

Eroticism, as Senf claims, is not the only trait of the female vampire. Other characteristics are rebellion and bloodsucking. All of these features are not only feared in the vampire but also in traditional women as well. This is due to the fact that they were expected to nurture other people, not suck their blood from them (see Senf 207). On this note, it is not surprising that the female vampire represents an exceptional threat to mankind.

3.1. Elisabeth Báthory, a 'Real' Vampire

Today, there are two historical persons who are associated with vampirism. The first one is Count Vlad Dracul (1431 – 1476), a Transylvanian ruler, who owes his epithet 'the Impaler' to his favourite method of execution. The second one is the Hungarian Countess Elisabeth Báthory (1560 – 1614) (see Flocke 10-11). According to the legend, the countess was very sensitive, so, when her maid combed Báthory's hair, she had to be careful not to hurt her. When servants were inapt nevertheless, the Countess would punish them. It so happened that once she hit a maid so hard that the latter bled from her head and mouth. A

---

[1] The topic of blood as an abject substance will be discussed in chapter 7.2.

drop of the blood landed on the Countess' hand and when she wanted to wipe it away, she was astonished to see that it had given her a healthier complexion than before. The incident caused her to think that more human blood would make her ageing body white like alabaster (see Farin 17). In order to maintain eternal youth and beauty with the help of their blood, Countess Báthory is said to have killed six hundred girls (see Flocke 10, 11), a deed that earned her the byname 'Blood Countess' (see Day 13). She may have been an inspiration for Le Fanu in creating the female vampire Carmilla in his novella of the same name. Not only does Carmilla drink the blood of her primarily female victims, she also sleeps in a coffin immersed in blood, which sustains her existence (see Le Fanu 134 ff.).

3.2. The Lesbian Vampire in Literature

The lesbian vampire as a literary protagonist surfaced in the late eighteenth century with Coleridge's unfinished poem *Christabel* (1817). The lesbian vampire has been depicted in numerous ways over the centuries and the aims of the stories have changed as well. Coleridge started to work on his aforementioned poem in 1797, and it was published in 1817. In it, a serpent-like woman, Geraldine, seduces the "lovely lady" (Coleridge 4) Christabel. According to Flocke, Geraldine represents the demonic element that threatens chaste Christian values (see Flocke 51). In the poem, Christabel has left her father's castle at midnight and is in the woods preying for her own knight. There she meets the aristocrat Geraldine who claims to have been seized from her father's side by five men the day before (see Coleridge 8-9). Christabel at once cares for the other woman and takes her with her to her room. Before they enter the castle, however, Geraldine faints, and Christabel carries her over the threshold herself, adding a biblical element to the poem (see Coleridge 11). Her guest swoons again when she sees the statue of an angel in Christabel's room (see Coleridge 14). The girls undress and Christabel is enchanted with Geraldine's body:

> Beneath the lamp the lady bow'd,
> And slowly roll'd her eyes around;
> Then drawing in her breath aloud,
> Like one that shuddered, she unbound
> The cincture from beneath her breast:
> Her silken robe, and inner vest,
> Dropt to her feet, and full in view,
> Behold! her bosom, and half her side——
> A sight to dream of, not to tell !
> And she is to sleep by Christabel.
> (Coleridge 17-8)

The next day Christabel becomes lethargic and weak while Geraldine appears to be stronger and more lively. In the end, Christabel is abandoned by Geraldine.

Sheridan Le Fanu based his novella *Carmilla* (1872) on Coleridge's poem (see Flocke 57). Like Christabel, Laura, the young protagonist of Le Fanu's work, gets to know the young girl Carmilla at night, and when her father agrees, Carmilla becomes their guest. Both Christabel and Laura lost their mothers when they were little, and both are seduced by a female vampire. Carmilla, according to Palmer, is punished in the end for the seduction of Laura with her death (see Palmer 100). Keesey claims that the novella served as an inspiration to the majority of lesbian vampire short stories and movies during the early 1970s (see Keesey 13). These films will not be discussed in this paper; *Carmilla*, however, will be dealt with in more detail in chapter 4.

The stigmatization of lesbian vampires proceeds in the twentieth century with D. H. Lawrence's novel *The Rainbow* (1915). It depicts the relationship between a female schoolteacher, Winifred Inger, and the protagonist Ursula. Their lovemaking leads to the latter's feeling a "heavy, clogged sense of deadness [...] from the other woman's contact" (Lawrence 333, see Palmer 101) and the vampiric portrayal of Inger as a predator is furthered by likening her to "a prehistoric lizard" (Palmer 101):

She still adhered to Winifred Inger. But a sort of nausea was coming over her. She loved her mistress. [...] And sometimes she thought Winifred was ugly, clayey. Her female hips seemed big and earthy, her ankles and her arms were too thick. She wanted some fine intensity, instead of this heavy cleaving of moist clay, that cleaves because it has no life of its own. (Lawrence 333)

Whitley Strieber's novel *The Hunger* (1981) also features a lesbian vampire, Miriam Blaylock, who, despite being portrayed as cruel and monstrous, at the same time signifies female power. Like Carmilla's relationship with Laura, Miriam's homo-erotic relations present a threat not only to the power men want to wield on female sexuality but also to the institution of marriage. The novel will be discussed in more detail in chapter 6.

Another novel featuring a lesbian vampire is *I, Vampire* (1984) by Jody Scott. It follows the existence of the narrator Sterling O'Blivion, who recounts her life and experiences from her birth in the Middle Ages to the twentieth century (see Palmer 1). The vampire in the novel functions as a spokesperson for the difficulties and pleasures of lesbian life. Scott uses humour and parody, e.g. the alien from outer space Benaroya, who meets Sterling disguised as Virginia Woolf[2], as a means to address and propagate issues concering sexual politics (see Palmer 105-6).

Katherine Forrest's *O Captain, My Captain* (1987) transforms the vampire narrative from a horror tale to a celebration of lesbian love. Her lesbian vampire is not a predator living on human love, but she becomes a "signifier of a feminine erotic economy" (Palmer 115).

The Gilda Stories (1991) is a novel by Jewelle Gomez that centres around the African-American lesbian vampire Gilda, the protagonist, and the events she experiences alone as well as with her friends, other black or coloured people. Thereby not only lesbian love is portrayed but also male homosexuality and bisexuality; the emphasis, however, lies on lesbian experience. What makes

---

[2] It is not surprising that Scott chose Virginia Woolf as the alien's preferred disguise, since she signifies lesbian love and female creativity (see Palmer 106).

Gomez's treatment of the lesbian vampire special, according to Palmer, is the interaction between the discourses of gender, sexual orientation and race (see Palmer 119). The Gilda Stories will be discussed in greater detail in chapter 6.

Of course, there are many more novels as well as short stories[3] featuring a lesbian vampire, but not all of them are treated in this thesis. The aforementioned novels have been chosen as illustrative examples of texts which depict the transformation of the lesbian vampire from the late eighteenth to twentieth century.

---

[3] Two anthologies that feature short stories about lesbian vampires and other creatures are, for instance, *Daughters of Darkness: Lesbian Vampire Tales* (1993) and *Bending the Landscape: Horror* (2003).

4. Sheridan Le Fanu's *Carmilla*

4.1. *The New Vampire in* Carmilla

> But I was not comforted,
> for I knew the visit of the strange woman
> was *not* a dream;
> and I was *awfully* frightened.
> (Laura in *Carmilla*, 75)

The year 1816 marks the birth of the vampire in literary life with Lord Byron's *Fragment of a Novel*, in which he introduces Augustus Darvell, a man – the word vampire is not yet mentioned – who accompanies the narrator on a journey through countries in the south of Europe and in the East (see Auerbach 1). In Lord Byron's fragment both men "had been educated at the same schools and university" (Byron 2). So, although the narrator senses that Darvell seems to have evil character traits (see Byron 3), he can relate to him nevertheless due to their similar upbringing. This changes with the introduction of Lord Ruthven in John Polidori's short story *The Vampyre* three years later (see Auerbach 1). Although both vampires are travelling companions to their human friends, the depiction of the latter suggests that Lord Ruthven may not be entirely human: although the "form and outline [of his face] were beautiful" (Polidori 7), he features a "dead grey eye [...] [and a] deadly hue of his face" (7). Yet, "the female sex [is] [not] indifferent to him" (7). In 1845, James Malcolm Rymer goes one step further in his novel *Varney the Vampyre, or, the Feast of Blood*. His vampire does not bear any resemblance to a human being anymore. Unlike the vampires described before, he is not friendly with humans, he preys on them, or, more precisely, he preys on "a girl young and beautiful as a spring morning" (Rymer 27). "The figure [...] [has] long nails, [...] a long gaunt hand, which seems utterly destitute of flesh" (29). Its face

> is perfectly white – perfectly bloodless. The eyes look like polished tin; the lips are drawn back, and the principal feature next to those dreadful eyes is the teeth – the fearful-looking teeth – projecting like those of

some wild animal, hideously, glaringly white, and fang-like. It approaches the bed with a strange, gliding movement. (Rymer 29)

Sheridan Le Fanu introduces a new vampire in his novella *Carmilla* in 1872. She is an "individualized [female] vampire" (Auerbach 46), who is depicted as an innocent young girl and whom the reader does not recognise as a vampire at first (see Beresford 125). Unlike the inhuman figure described in *Varney,* the vampire in *Carmilla* is not a stranger to her victim (see Auerbach 42). The two female protagonists of the story, Carmilla and Laura, get to know each other and eventually become friends. They not only share dreams but also a lost mother (see Auerbach 43). Furthermore, there is nothing mysterious about the girl Carmilla. She is described as a beautiful young girl who does not have fangs, she does not hypnotize Laura when she looks into her eyes (see Auerbach 45). She does, however, have pointed elongated teeth. Yet, Laura does not notice them herself, her attention is called to Carmilla's teeth by a hunchback (see Le Fanu 94). Furthermore, there are no mysterious oaths between vampires and humans in *Carmilla.* Unlike the dying Lord Ruthven, who makes Aubrey swear to keep his existence a secret (see Polidori 17), Carmilla does not make Laura keep any secrets. But it is Carmilla's mother by whom she is sworn not to disclose anything about her family and origin. She does, however, openly declare her affection towards her host numerous times. The female vampire's story is not one of predation but rather one of friendship and love (see Auerbach 42). Palmer points out that while Darvell and Lord Ruthven stay friends with their male companions, Carmilla gives in to her desires and passionately shows her affection to the object of her desire, Laura. She does so through the way she looks at the girl, but also through her actions, which sometimes can be classified as sexual (see Palmer 100). Carmilla loves her prey, while the male vampires before her saw their prey solely as food (see Auerbach 18). She does prey on peasant girls, yet she falls in love with Laura, who, like her, comes from a protected family background (see Auerbach 41)[4]. As mentioned before, Augustus Darvell and Lord Ruthven travel the world with their human companions; Carmilla, on the other hand, seduces her friends in

---

[4] Carmilla's and Laura's relationship will be discussed in more detail in chapter 4.2.1.

the obscure privacy of women's bedrooms and dreams (see Gelder 64). Another difference between Polidori's and Le Fanu's stories is that blood is not as important in the latter as it is in the first. *The Vampyre* presents a bloody portrayal of the vampire's attack: "upon [the victim's] neck and breast was blood, and upon her throat were the marks of teeth having opened the vein" (Polidori 15). Likewise, Varney's assault is brutal and gory: "[w]ith a plunge he seizes her neck in his fang-like teeth – a gush of blood, and a hideous sucking noise follows" (Rymer 30). When the vampire is discovered, he is described as "one who has to renew a dreadful existence by human blood – one who lives on for ever, and must keep up such a fearful existence upon human gore – one who eats not and drinks not as other men" (35). However, when Carmilla's last victim Laura details her nightly dreams, she speaks of "[a] pleasant, peculiar cold thrill which we feel in bathing, when we move against the current of a river" (Le Fanu 105). Again, what Laura experiences is nothing unsettling or mysterious. Like Carmilla, the act of swimming is familiar to her, therefore, she is not afraid of her nightly experiences (see Auerbach 44). But blood does become important at the end of the novella, when Carmilla, unmasked as a vampire by General Vordenburg, is found immersed in a "leaden coffin floated with blood [...] [in] a depth of seven inches" (Le Fanu 134). The liquid is the only physical evidence of Carmilla's otherness since her appearance is that of a sleeping human: "Her eyes were open; no cadaverous smell exhaled from the coffin. [...] [T]here was a faint, but appreciable respiration, and a corresponding action of the heart. The limbs were perfectly flexible, the flesh elastic" (134). With regard to blood, another difference between Carmilla and the male vampires preceding her is how the vampire takes blood from his or her victims. It has been pointed out that both Polidori's vampire and Rymer's Varney feed from the neck. Laura, however, experiences "a sensation as if two needles ran into [her] breast very deep at the same moment" when she first meets Carmilla in her dream as a child (74). As an adult she mentions the same feeling connected to her bosom when she dreams of being visited by a large cat in the night. Similarly, Carmilla points to her breast when she alludes to Laura how she was turned into a vampire many years ago (see Le Fanu 101).

4.2. The Threat of the Lesbian Vampire in Carmilla

> "she talked like a friend;
> she admired her dress,
> and insinuated very prettily her admiration of her beauty."
> (General Spielsdorf in Carmilla, 119)

4.2.1.   The Lesbian Vampire as a Threat to Male Dominance

The friendship between Laura and the vampire Carmilla is, as already mentioned, a new feature in vampire fiction. It comes about because Laura grows up in a remote castle somewhere in Styria, with only her father and two governesses as companions. When Carmilla enters her life, she represents not only the much needed friend of supposedly the same age, but also someone who she has a lot in common with (see Auerbach 43). According to Auerbach, Carmilla is "Laura's only available source of intimacy" (38). Both girls are motherless since Laura's mother died when she was a baby and Carmilla's mother left to do some business in another country. They even share a common dream in Laura's childhood, in which they both perceive the other one as "a young lady", not as a child (Le Fanu, 74, 86). Laura's mother even appears in what the girl thinks must be a dream, when in reality she is indeed attacked by Carmilla. Laura hears a voice telling her that "[her] mother warns [her] to beware of the assassin" (106). When the girl awakens frightened, she sees Carmilla bathed in blood in her room. Despite the evidence, she believes that the voice warns her not of Carmilla, but of somebody attacking the latter. That means that mother and lover as well as attacker and murdered fuse into one. And the men, who analyse the situation, do not realise that (see Auerbach 43). Carmilla thinks of her meeting Laura again as destiny and asks her: "I have never had a friend—shall I find one now?" (Le Fanu 87). The girls become friends quickly and Carmilla shows her adoration for Laura openly:

> She used to place her pretty arms about my neck, draw me to her, and laying her cheek to mine, murmur with her lips near my ear, "Dearest, your little heart is wounded; think me not cruel because I obey the

irresistible law of my strength and weakness; if your dear heart is wounded, my wild heart bleeds with yours. In the rapture of my enormous humiliation I live in your warm life, and you shall die—die, sweetly die— into mine." [...] And when she had spoken such a rhapsody, she would press me more closely in her trembling embrace, and her lips in soft kisses gently glow upon my cheek. (Le Fanu 89)

Carmilla is explicit about her feelings towards the girl through embraces, touches, blushing and other gestures. Her behaviour is appropriate within the framework of romantic friendship between women in the nineteenth century. At first, Laura considers Carmilla's acting as friendship, and she later recollects: "Young people like, and even love, on impulse. I was flattered by the evident, though as yet undeserved, fondness she showed me. I liked the confidence with which she at once received me. She was determined that we should be dear friends" (Le Fanu 87). Then Laura's feelings become ambiguous. On the one hand, she feels "'drawn towards her,' but there [is] also something of repulsion" (87). Even when Laura and her family approach Carmilla's carriage, they do so "in curiosity and horror" (79). This dichotomy is stressed repeatedly. When Carmilla's declarations of love become more frequent, Laura does not understand Carmilla's emotions or utterances (see Le Fanu 89). Her ambiguous feelings, however, increase (see O'Malley 140):

I experienced a strange tumultuous excitement that was pleasurable, ever and anon, mingled with a vague sense of fear and disgust. I had no distinct thoughts about her while such scenes lasted, but I was conscious of a love growing into adoration, and also of abhorrence. This I know is a paradox, but I can make no other attempt to explain the feeling. (Le Fanu 90)

Laura's lack of understanding may be due to the fact that Carmilla's love is different from the love a friend would show her. Her motifs are more like those of a lover, and Laura is embarrassed by that. Since she cannot come up with a satisfactory explanation for Carmilla's behaviour, she suspects that her friend is actually a boy in disguise (see Le Fanu 91). But she counters that "[e]xcept in these brief periods of mysterious excitement her ways were girlish; and there was always a languor about her, quite incompatible with a masculine system in a state of health" (Le Fanu 91). Laura even notices that the more her own health declines, the more affectionate Carmilla becomes (see Le Fanu 105). Trying to find reasonable explanations, the girl even refers Carmilla's behaviour to momentary insanity (see Le Fanu 105). But it is also important to note that Carmilla's attempts at seducing Laura are successful, for the girl's dream features erotic images, which she is too innocent to recognise (see Senf 205):

> Sometimes there came a sensation as if a hand was drawn softly along my cheek and neck. Sometimes it was as if warm lips kissed me, and longer and more lovingly as they reached my throat, but there the caress fixed itself. My heart beat faster, my breathing rose and fell rapidly and full drawn; a sobbing, that rose into a sense of strangulation, supervened, and turned into a dreadful convulsion, in which my senses left me, and I became unconscious (Le Fanu 105-6).

Laura experiences feelings that can be compared to those of a climax. She does not, however, connect that to Carmilla, but rather to the illness that has befallen her. Similarly to being attracted to Carmilla, she is also attracted to the disease that the latter brings about, at least at first (see O'Malley 141):

> Without knowing it, I was now in a pretty advanced stage of the strangest illness under which mortal ever suffered. There was an unaccountable fascination in its earlier symptoms that more than reconciled me to the incapacitating effect of that stage of the malady. This fascination increased for a time, until it reached a certain point, when gradually a sense of the horrible mingled itself with it, deepening, [...], until it discoloured and perverted the whole state of my life". (Le Fanu 105)

Laura's love for Carmilla continues even after she has gained knowledge of the latter's true identity. The way the girl accounts the vampire's dispatch seems almost like a prosaic anticlimax compared to the lovely descriptions of their blooming friendship and love (see Auerbach, 46; see Le Fanu 134). This is due to the fact that Laura was not allowed to attend the vampire's killing. She gathered her information from a report of the Imperial Commission (see Le Fanu 135). Yet, she states that thinking about the events from several years distance, they still evoked anxiety in her: "I write all this you suppose with composure. But far from it; I cannot think of it without agitation. Nothing but your earnest desire so repeatedly expressed, could have induced me to sit down to a task that has unstrung my nerves for months to come" (Le Fanu 135). Also, Laura's definition of 'the vampire' pales next to the elaborate depiction of her conversations and experiences with Carmilla. She describes the vampire's advances as follows:

> The vampire is prone to be fascinated with an engrossing vehemence, resembling the passion of love, by particular persons. In pursuit of these it will exercise inexhaustible patience and stratagem [...]. It will never desist until it has satiated its passion, and drained the very life of its coveted victim. But it will, in these cases, husband and protract its murderous enjoyment with the refinement of an epicure, and heighten it by the gradual approaches of an artful courtship. In these cases it seems to yearn for something like sympathy and consent. In ordinary ones it goes direct to its object, overpowers with violence, and strangles and exhausts often at a single feast. (Le Fanu 136)

This depiction shows that the girl is aware of the fact that she meant more to Carmilla than most of her other victims did. Their relationship was not based on the vampire's necessity to feed only. Maybe this is the reason why even after Carmilla's death, she has ambiguous memories of her as "sometimes the playful, languid, beautiful girl; sometimes the writhing fiend [she] saw in the ruined church" (Le Fanu 137). Her lingering warm feelings for Carmilla become obvious when she states: "and often from a reverie I have started, fancying I heard the light step of Carmilla at the drawing-room door" (137).

Carmilla, on the other hand, describes her own murder and eventual turn into a vampire as an act of love: "Yes, a very – cruel love – strange love, that would have taken my life. Love will have its sacrifices. No sacrifice without blood" (Le Fanu 101). This indicates that she really does love Laura. To her, her nightly visits and the taking of Laura's blood are not meant as a harm but are a token of her, albeit unusual, love for the girl. Carmilla, the lesbian vampire, poses a threat to the moral values of Victorian societies (see Palmer 100) and to the men in the story, since she signifies female power and challenges the institution of marriage (see Palmer 101). In order to restore order, the men in the story need to kill her. Therefore, it is important to analyse them as well.

4.2.2. Female Protagonists – Male Paranoia

Le Fanu's novella *Carmilla* was written and published in the second half of the nineteenth century, at a time when people had clear ideas about what they considered was feminine and masculine. Women were related to the private sphere, the family and the home, whereas the men's domain was the public one (see Parker 11). As Parker states, "feminity and masculinity in the wrong sex were regarded as a misfortune, undermining the integrity of the character" (11). In this light, according to Gelder, *Carmilla* can be read as an anti patriarchal novella (see Gelder 54). As already mentioned, it centres around the two female protagonists Laura and Carmilla. The former presents her story as part of a case study carried out by Dr. Hesselius. It deals with her friendship with Carmilla and her finding out about the latter's existence as a vampire, and the events that lead to the discovery. It is the men in the story who diagnose Laura's case and the vampire outside of the girl's hearing range (see Gelder 49). Although they seem to mean well by trying to shield her from their conversations and their frightful contents, it is their patronising behaviour that allows for events to unfold that almost lead to Laura's death.

The first of the diagnosing men is Laura's father, a widower, who attempts to trace back the source of his daughter's declining health to natural causes (Le Fanu 94). He does not believe in supernatural beings and does not change his attitude even after General Spielsdorf implies that he himself once was like Laura's father, but "[he] ha[s] learned better" (115). He is amused by monsters (93) and, as Willis states, is unable to recognise the signs of vampiric activity. Although he consults a doctor, he ridicules the man, who, after having examined Laura, suggests a vampire as source of the girl's advancing mysterious disease (see Willis 117): "Well, I do wonder at a wise man like you. What do you say to hippogriffs and dragons?" (Le Fanu 96). Even when he learns about vampires from yet another man, Doctor Spielsberg, he puts off Laura's queries for the cause of her disease. And again, after General Spielsdorf has related the circumstances that led to his niece's death, a story remarkably similar to what Laura and her father had experienced, he holds back information from Laura. She knows that "it was clear that it was a secret which [her] father for the present determined to keep from [her]" (133).

The other man in the story who guards his niece Bertha and Carmilla, who then called herself Millarca, is General Spielsberg. Like Laura's father, he does not connect Mircalla to his niece's sickness. He is equally convinced that vampires originate in superstition. He also sends for two doctors for help; these two, however, get into an argument over the source of Bertha's illness. One of the physicians, having been made fun of by the other, leaves a letter explaining that the girl suffers from the aftermath of a vampire's attack. Even upon seeing the diagnosis documented in black and white, the General "[is himself] wholly sceptical as to the existence of any such portent as the vampire [...] [and] the supernatural theory of the good doctor furnished, in [his] opinion, but another instance of learning and intelligence oddly associated with some one hallucination" (Le Fanu 130). Yet, out of sheer despair, he chooses to act upon the doctor's letter in order to help her, but his ward dies nevertheless.

Doctor Spielsberg, who has already been mentioned, is the next man who literally examines and diagnoses Laura. He is called by Laura's father because the illness that has befallen her, which she has tried to keep a secret, has become visible in her face (Le Fanu 106). The doctor seems to know that a vampire is the source behind Laura's symptoms, yet again, he does not tell her. He converses with her father instead, both men look grave and although Laura senses that her situation is worrisome and she asks the men what is wrong with her, Doctor Spielsberg soothes her by saying "Nothing, my dear young lady [...]" (112). When she continues to ask whether there is any danger, he again negates her question. Furthermore, although he asks Madame to stay with Laura at any time, he does not explain to the woman the reasons behind his order. The men's behaviour does nothing but keep the women in the story ignorant of the danger Laura is in. It is interesting to note that it is Carmilla who dismisses the male authority of the physicians: "Doctors never did me any good" (95).

Baron Vordenburg is another man evaluating the vampire Carmilla. He draws a plan of the chapel in which Carmilla later is found in her coffin, and he owns a great number of books about vampires. It is his studies that give Laura insight into the topic of the vampire; she refers to them in her account for Dr. Hesselius' case study[5]. Another man who is consulted by the General during the men's search for Carmilla is the woodman. He speaks about revenants and vampires and tells a story about yet another man, a Moravian noble, who once killed a vampire and was then assigned with the task of removing the tomb of Mircalla (see Le Fanu 127-8). Gelder refers to Copjec and states that a signifier can never designate itself (see Gelder 50; see Copjec 13). That is why the men in *Carmilla* do so. "In order to signify the vampire", they form a "bureaucracy without end" (Gelder 50), that comes into being and that hears testimonies of the same kind over and over again. Despite all the evidence for the workings of a vampire, the men need further proof and hear repeated versions of the same testimony. When they do signify Carmilla as vampire, they can eventually destroy her (see Gelder 49). Laura puts that into words in the story:

> If human testimony, taken with every care and solemnity, judicially, before commissions innumerable, each consisting of many members, all chosen for integrity and intelligence, and constituting reports more voluminous perhaps that exist upon any one other class of cases, is worth anything, it is difficult to deny, or even to doubt the existence of such a phenomenon as the vampire. (Le Fanu 134)

As already mentioned, according to Gelder, the men form one of these commissions in order to make sense of the vampire and, as a consequence, be able to get rid of it in the end (see Gelder 50). It is interesting that the father in the story, who had a ward to protect, does not believe in vampires. He is, as Gelder puts it, "mobilised by much older men who are shown to have had [a] kind of close proximity to vampires [...]" (Gelder 54). One of these men is

---

[5] *Carmilla* is one in a collection of five tales that are loosely connected and are presented as the case files of Dr. Martin Hesselius.

General Spielsdorf, whose "dear wife was maternally descended from the Karnsteins" (Le Fanu 116). The next one is the Moravian nobleman, who "had been a passionate and favoured lover of the beautiful Mircalla, Countess Karnstein" (136). The woodman represents the people who have lived in the area close to the Karnstein castle all their lives. Finally, there is Baron Vordenburg, who does extensive studies on vampires (see Gelder 54).

Women play important roles in *Carmilla*. The protagonist of the story and the evil, albeit loved, villain are female. So is, as Auerbach states, the vampire who created Carmilla (see Auerbach 40). When Carmilla speaks of how she was turned, she uses the word 'strange', which Auerbach claims, can be read as "Swinburnian euphemism for homosexual love" (Auerbach 40). *Carmilla* is a story in which the men try to retain the upper hand in their quest to destroy a woman. The men who are responsible for allowing Carmilla/Mircalla to enter their homes consequently endanger their wards and thus lose their power over them. They are cleverly persuaded to do so by Carmilla's mother, another woman, who is described as a lady "with a commanding air and figure" (Le Fanu 80). She cleverly orchestrates the plots which, subsequently, lead to her daughter's reception at their victims' houses. It has been noted above that the men do their diagnosing among themselves only, excluding the women. Likewise, though, the exchanges between Carmilla and Laura, and Carmilla and Bertha, also take place without male participation (see Signorotti 607). According to Flocke, the two girls represent two different approaches to female sexuality (see Flocke 60). The first one, Carmilla, shows rampant sexual desire, whereas the other one, Laura, is morally chaste. Both of them, however, are dominated by men. Due to male intervention, Laura does not get to realise that she desires Carmilla sexually, and Carmilla is overpowered and, finally, killed before her actions can kill her beloved one (see Flocke 60).

It is interesting to note that one of Laura's governesses, Mademoiselle, sees "a hideous black woman, with a sort of coloured turban on her head [...] [and] with gleaming eyes and large white eye-balls, and her teeth set as if in fury" (Le

Fanu 83). The General, however, notes that Mircalla's mother took orders from "a gentleman, dressed in black, who looked particularly elegant and distinguished, with this drawback, that his face was the most deadly pale [he] ever saw, except in death" (120). In doing so, the General restores male authority (see Auerbach 46).

4.2.3. The Lesbian Vampire as a Threat to Victorian Moral Concepts

In his book *Reading the Vampire* (1994), Gelder draws attention to Eve Kosofsky Sedgwick's concept of the erotic triangle in Gothic novels (see Gelder 59). The triangle is made up of two male rivals and one woman. The bond between the men is as strong, or even stronger, than the one between either of the rivals and his beloved. Also, it is not homosexual, but homo-social. Gelder claims that the woman's role in that mixture of links is not that of an equal partner, she is rather "an object of exchange between the already-bonded men" (60). In *Carmilla*, the roles are reversed. Here, the three components in the triangle are two women, a daughter and a guest, and a group of men, fathers and paternal figures. The very re-alignment of the triangle poses a threat to the fathers. Furthermore, Carmilla is not only a woman, but she is, as Gelder states, a queer woman (see Gelder 60), who drains their daughters until they are dead.

It has been noted in chapter 4.2.2. that during the Victorian era it was the private sphere that was linked to women. The ideal woman was seen as the Angel in the House, a term that was coined in the title of a poem by Coventry Patmore from 1845. The attributes desired in women in the nineteenth century were virtue, innocence, passivity, dependence, self-sacrifice, love, compassion and beauty. She was not, however, considered to be a sexual human being (see Christ 146-7). It is not surprising, then, that the men in *Carmilla* feel threatened both by Carmilla and her mother. It must have been rather unusual for a woman of the era in question to abandon her child and leave it in the care of strangers for several weeks at a time, be it a mission of life and death or not. Nevertheless, the General agrees to take care of Carmilla during her mother's absence, although he later confesses that he "submitted" because he felt "quite overpowered" (Le Fanu 122). Women in the nineteenth century were thought to need male protection. By appealing to the General, and later to the father's sense of honour, the mother manages to turn chivalry into a weakness (see Signorotti 616).

Carmilla also poses a threat to the institution of marriage. Her father wishes that "the General [...] had chosen any other time" (Le Fanu 113) to visit them, a time when Laura had been better. Yet, the girl's disease, visible in her countenance, and furthermore inflicted by Carmilla, upsets his plans (see Signorotti 616). The men's only way to eliminate the threat is to kill Carmilla. This, however, proves to be a more difficult venture than the General had at first imagined. When he hides in the room of his dying niece, he observes Carmilla's deadly visit. Yet, he cannot intervene as he is excluded from Carmilla's and Bertha's exchange, one that is completely outside of the boundaries stipulated by tradition, as an onlooker (see Signorotti 615). Once more male authority is undermined by a female. Furthermore, even though the vampire is eliminated in the end, the men's endeavours are made futile by Laura's last comment in her account, in which she "[fancies] [she] heard the light step of Carmilla at the drawing-room door" (Le Fanu 137).

The story, however, as Gelder states, does not condemn Carmilla. On the contrary, sympathy is elicited in various ways (see Gelder 61). Lesbianism was seen as unnatural in the Victorian era, as against Nature. An indication of this is the illness that spreads in Laura and the adjoining village (see Gelder 61). When two peasant girls die shortly one after the other, one having seen a ghost and the other having been seized by her throat, Laura thinks of a plague or a fever that overtakes the country (see Le Fanu 92). Her father refers the illnesses to natural causes and regards local superstition as an infection (see Willis 112). He asks two physicians for help when Laura falls ill and declares that God is the only one who can help them. However, Carmilla, interestingly, refers the disease to nature (see Le Fanu 95). Unlike Laura, who simply accepts her father's theories, Carmilla has a voice and she expresses her own opinion. She refuses to believe in God because she generally rejects "to include males in her exclusively female kinship system" (Signorotti 616). Instead, she believes in Mother Nature, another female entity. She even indicates that her relationship with Laura is natural (see Signorotti 616): "All things proceed from Nature – don't they? All things in the heaven, in the earth, and under the earth, act and live as Nature ordains? I think so" (Le Fanu 95). Laura might not be of the same opinion. She compares her feelings for Carmilla to a fascination that kept growing "until it discoloured and perverted the whole state of [her] life" (105). Thus, she likenes her admiration and love to a perversion, something unnatural, since she cannot reasonably explain them.

The hunchback, the only one who notices Carmilla's sharp, thin, long and pointed tooth, sells both girls a charm against the oupire, i.e. the vampire, who is responsible for the deaths. Yet, Carmilla's explanation to Laura about the amulet's charm is a medical one again. According to her, it is immersed in an antidote against malaria (see Le Fanu 104). Even in the end, Carmilla's elimination is likened to riddening the country of a plague (see Willis 112).

It is not only the two vampires that jeopardise the male authority. Even Laura does so by not telling her father about Carmilla's frightening behaviour (see Signorotti 614). Signorotti also claims that even the layout of the story frees the two protagonists from male control. Although the prologue by Doctor Hesselius' assistant mentions a note by the physician himself attached to the story, it as well as the editor's epilogue are missing. Signorotti reads that as a sign of another failed attempt of the male to supervise the female. Moreover, Laura addresses "a town lady like you" (Le Fanu 91), thus establishing a link between her and the female reader and at the same time abolishing the link to the male readers (see Signorotti 619).

4.2.4.　　One Woman's Blood is Another Man's Poison

Interestingly, the vampire is perceived differently by Laura, who is herself a victim to the vampire's visits while she sleeps, and by General Spielsdorf, who witnesses Mircalla's attack on his niece, Bertha Rheinfeldt. Laura does not perceive Carmilla as a threat and as the source behind the nightly assaults because the latter is familiar to her. That is why she reports of a cat that attacks her in her dream as an adult:

> [I]t was very dark, and I saw something moving round the foot of the bed, which at first I could not accurately distinguish. But I soon saw that it was a sooty-black animal that resembled a monstrous cat. It appeared to me about four or five feet long, for it measured fully the length of the hearth-rug as it passed over; and it continued to-ing and fro-ing with the lithe sinister restlessness of a beast in a cage. (Le Fanu 102)

After the attack Laura sees "a female figure" (Le Fanu 102) in her room. Likewise, she describes being soothed by a young lady as a child, an incident that ended with the first attack on her (see Le Fanu 74). Even after the General has told his story, and the evidence points towards Carmilla as the villain, she has nothing but friendly words for her: "I saw very gladly the beautiful face and figure of Carmilla enter the shadowy chapel" (Le Fanu 131). The General, however, does not identify a woman as the attacker of his niece. He sees "a large black object, very ill-defined, crawl, as it seemed to me, over the foot of the bed, and swiftly spread itself up to the poor girl's throat, where it swelled, in a moment, into a great, palpitating mass" (130). When he recovers from the shock, he clearly identifies Millarca as the perpetrator though (see Le Fanu 130). These differences in perception may be rooted in the differing relationships with the attacker Carmilla/Mircalla. As already mentioned in chapter 4.2.1., Laura is fond of Carmilla and even calls her a friend. Despite Carmilla's love-stricken advances, there is nothing in her behaviour that should alarm Laura. The General's motifs, on the other hand, are different from Laura's. He acts as Bertha's guardian, and although, like his nice, Mircalla is his ward, he recognises her in his niece's bedroom. This may be due to the fact that he does not have a friendly relationship with her.

5. Whitley Strieber's *The Hunger*

5.1 The Female Vampire in The Hunger

> The perfect predator would be
> indistinguishable from his prey.
> (Strieber 228)

In 1981, Whitley Strieber introduced the bisexual vampire Miriam Blaylock, who is the last of an ancient, alien species (see Senf 202). To Miriam, the sex of her companions is "a matter of indifference" (Strieber 73). The book, however, focuses on her seduction of the scientist Dr. Sarah Roberts. Like Carmilla, she knows how to seduce her victims, and like Elisabeth Báthory, she uses blood to give her immortality (see Creed 67). She is described as beautiful and fragrant by those who love her, and by humans who see her for the first time (see Strieber 16, 154, 166, 309). Yet, her beauty is the product of careful makeup and a wig (see Strieber 25). To those who Miriam has changed and turned into vampiric beings, her appearance without makeup is beyond words (see Strieber 347). Humans who are afraid of her and her immortal companions who are not on good terms with her anymore, perceive her odour as a smell of decay (see Strieber 16, 95, 166, 240). Like Carmilla and other vampires before her, Miriam has enhanced senses like sharp hearing and acute sense of smell (see Strieber 119, 134). Also, she enjoys the act of killing (see Strieber 7) and can herself be destroyed by a wooden stake driven through her heart (see Strieber 262). Her blood, though, shows anomalies and her brain is "like a dead brain that's somehow retaining consciousness" (Strieber 174). Like Carmilla, she is not confined to the hours of the night (see Strieber 134), she is, however, bound by Sleep, a "deep revitalizing trance peculiar to [her] kind" (Strieber 19). Miriam's species needs to sleep six hours each day; it is vital and, when it comes, it cannot be delayed. "Almost as absolute as death, it [is] the key to the renewal of life" (38). Unlike many other vampires, Miriam does not need fangs. As sharp as a scalpel, it is her tongue that penetrates human flesh and opens arteries for her to suck the blood from (see Strieber 302). She does not take sips of blood, though, she dries her victims completely of their blood leaving "dark lumpy thing[s]" (Strieber 5). Yet, Miriam provides justification for her predatory behaviour (see Pharr 99): "She had identified her own animal ancestors. She belonged to mankind and mankind to her, just as the saber-toothed tiger and the buffalo had once belonged to each other" (Strieber 133).

Strieber has also made his vampire utterly lonely. As the last of her race, she seeks eternal love and company. She chooses one companion at a time and lures them by promising them eternal life by her side (see Creed 67). Like Carmilla to Laura, Miriam becomes a close friend to her victims and she enjoys close intimacy with them (see Auerbach 59). Her assurance, however, is not entirely honest since her companions, transformed by transfusions of her blood into their body, start to age after a couple of centuries. They become crumbling creatures who are too weak to feed and, due to Miriam's blood in their system, cannot die. They are doomed to vegetate in caskets, which Miriam keeps in the attic. Thus, Strieber has created the exact opposite to the traditional vampire crypt that is usually situated in the cellar (see Creed 68). Although the fate that Miriam leaves her former lovers to is dreadful, her loneliness and desperation over it make her, similar to Carmilla, appealing nevertheless (see Senf 202).

Being the last one of her species has not only made Miriam lonely, it has also made her meticulous. Once her current companion shows symptoms of ageing, she already has a casket waiting for him or her in the attic. And as soon as she chooses a human who shall become her next companion, she carefully plans her or his seduction. Thereby, she does not like to leave anything to chance. Thus, she thoroughly studies her or his habits and character, schedules the first meeting and even memorises the outlay of her victim's apartment. Before she approaches Dr. Roberts in the clinic she works at, Miriam also rehearses for the interview there. When it comes to satisfying her hunger for blood, the accurateness can also be seen in the fact that her "first rule of survival [is] to take only the unwanted" (Strieber 119). That way she reduces the risk of being found by the police. Furthermore, she never leaves the remains of the bodies behind. Instead, she burns them in an oven in her house. She always does so before dawn so that the smoke will be gone before the sun rises (see Strieber 22). Next to the furnace room, Miriam's house also has an elaborate security system (see Strieber 262). It is that fortification that grants her security and freedom from being discovered and hunted by humans. When she sleeps, her bed is surrounded by steel shutters to prevent any harm from within the house. Miriam is even diligent in gardening. Her garden harbours her precious roses, "her own special hybrids, created over God knew how many years of patient grafting" (Strieber 189).

Miriam is also highly cautious. Despite her strength and immortality, in a car she "fasten[s] the seatbelt [...], lock[s] her door but leav[es] her hand near the catch in case it was necessary to exit quickly" (Strieber 133).

Another facility that Miriam uses to her advantage is the *touch*, a trait "she share[s] only with her own race, and some of the higher primates" (Strieber 64). It allows her to sense others like her (see Strieber 64), share emotions (see Strieber 119) and implant images in humans' minds (see Strieber 126). *Touching* is a useful device in Miriam's act of seduction since it arouses strong and positive emotions in her victims and helps her gain insight into their feelings for her.

Interestingly, humans triumph over the vampire in *The Hunger*, although it is the vampire who survives in the end. Miriam fails in her attempt to turn Sarah into her companion. The latter chooses vegetating in a box over eternal life with and like Miriam by slicing her wrists with a scalpel. The loss of blood leads to Sarah's body becoming like those of Miriam's lovers before her. Hence, Sarah retains her humanity and proves to be superior to the vampire (see Day 92, see Auerbach 59). And it is the love for her lover that allows Sarah to be content with her decision, albeit the horrible implications. Thus, the ending indicates that human love conquers all, even the alien promise of immortality. Also, the vampire acknowledges her failure: "But Miriam now realized that the gift she could confer was not above one such as Sarah, but beneath her. [...] No matter how her loneliness tempted her to find one who would last forever, she resolved never to attempt the transformation on another like Sarah, not this time or the next time, or for all time" (Strieber 356-7, see Day 92).

5.2. Miriam, the Threatening Lesbian Vampire in The Hunger

> I will keep you with me for all time.
> I will never abandon you,
> and you will always have a place in my heart.
> (Miriam in *The Hunger*, 357)

5.2.1. The Blood of the Vampire as Forbidden Fruit

In *The Hunger*, the vampire is not only a predator consuming her prey, she also becomes the forbidden fruit herself (see Pharr 100). Sarah is a scientist whose current project is to find a means to overcome ageing (see Strieber 52). For five years she has worked on an experiment with the ape Methuselah analysing the correlation between ageing and sleeping (see Strieber 54-5). When Sarah watches Methuselah's dying on a monitor, her first thought albeit the horror she has just witnessed is: "*We need not die*" (Strieber 75). To her, the ape's life "[is] a fair price for such an enormous gain to humanity" (Strieber 75). Hence, it is not surprising that she is tempted by Miriam's offer of at least doubling her life span (see Strieber 274). Miriam's blood is of utmost importance for the transformation process since it consumes the humans' blood and replaces it with cells of its own kind (see Strieber 259). Thus, it is not only human blood that plays an important role as nourishment for the vampire, but it is the vampire's blood which offers longevity and thus becomes the forbidden fruit. Before Sarah realizes that the price she has to pay for Miriam's gift is to sacrifice the love of her life, which she does by killing Tom, Sarah actually considers accepting the present. As a scientist she possesses an innate curiosity in defeating the process of ageing, she is driven by a hunger to find a cure. This yearning can be compared to Miriam's hunger for blood as a vampire. After Sarah finds out that Miriam has secretly drugged her and transfused her blood into Sarah's body, she finds the deed fearsome and horrifying. She analyses both her own blood as well as Miriam's and, manipulated by the latter, starts to see the advantages of the alien's life. This may also be due to the fact that in the novel vampirism is not only connected to youth but also to beauty (see Abbott 134). When Sarah meets Miriam for the first time in the clinic she "[finds] herself in the presence of something much more profound than physical beauty, and yet [she finds] the sheer magnificence of the woman's body and the serenity of her expression [...] remarkable" (Strieber 154). Also, when the transformed Sarah perceives Miriam in her true form, without the disguise of the makeup, she screams with

> delight wild beyond words. Miriam [does] not look a thing like a human being, but she [is] *beautiful!* [...] This [is] the Goddess Athena, Isis— Sarah [can] not find a name ... The eyes [are] not pale gray at all, but shining, golden, piercingly bright. The skin was as white and smooth as marble. There [are] no eyebrows, but the face [is] so noble, so much at peace that just seeing it [makes] Sarah want to sob out the petty passions of her own humanity and have done with them forever. The hair, which had been concealed by a wig, as gold as the eyes, [is] soft, almost like smoke, finer than the hair of a baby. Angel's hair. (Strieber 309)

Also, Miriam's chosen companions have all been good-looking before the ageing process started. Eumenes, her lover during the times of the Roman empire, was not only exceptionally strong but also handsome, and next to him "[h]er own beauty blossomed as never before" (Strieber 36). After his loss, Miriam is "staggered by [Lollia's] beauty" (177). When her current consort John shows symptoms of ageing, it is too soon for her since "she love[s] him so—his youth, his freshness" (19).

While in *Carmilla*, it is a disease instead of vampirism that is made responsible for the dying of the people, in *The Hunger* the process of ageing is likened to a disease (see Abbott 134). Even the vocabulary used is from the field of medicine. Hence, Sarah's job in the clinic is to find "the cure for man's most universal disease—old age" (Strieber 52). When John shows symptoms of ageing, Miriam hopes "to find an antidote" (70) for him. While her own body shows a permanent "immunity" (70), "Sleep only delay[s]" (70) ageing for her creatures for a while. But when Miriam transfuses her own blood into Sarah's body, it replaces Sarah's blood cells and will finally dominate them – like a disease, at least for a short time, takes control over a sick human's system. This means that the vampire's blood becomes a cure against human's disease of mortality (see Auerbach 178)

5.2.2.   Miriam Blaylock Threatens Sexual Status Quo

Dr. Sarah Roberts is in a relationship with Tom Havers, who, like her, works at the Riverside clinic. Although they occasionally have problems in their relationship, it nevertheless fulfils them sexually. Even when there is a certain distance between them and Sarah feels that there is something missing in her life, their sexuality is satisfying for both of them. Also, Sarah loves Tom and trusts him implicitly (see Strieber 117). Yet, she still falls prey to Miriam's lure. Miriam knows that Sarah and Tom find sexual pleasure with each other, still she believes that she is able to show the doctor what she really wants. She senses that something is missing in Sarah's life and she exploits her need for love: "Miriam could work in the forest of Sarah's emotions. She [knows] well her role in this age: the bringer of truth" (Strieber 163). The first change Miriam causes in Sarah is by *touching* her in her sleep and implanting "images of soft female flesh, smooth flesh, into Sarah's mind, making her writhe with longing" (126). Sarah is surprised by her own feelings and she finds it "disquieting to have dreamed with such lust of a woman" (127). Still, when she makes love to Tom later the next day, she thinks of the female bodies of her dream and she "experience[s] a moment of pleasure, rare and stunning" (128). When Miriam seeks help from Sarah in the clinic, she strips naked in the examination room, although she is only told to take off her blouse (see Strieber 156). When she sits down on the examination table, she spreads her leg wide so that Sarah can "actually smell the faint musky scent of the woman's vagina" (Strieber 157). During Sarah's examination of Miriam's body, "her nipples [are] erect [and] Sarah [is] transfixed" (158) with the perfection of her body. But Miriam does not stop there, she also makes the same noise she herself produces at the moment of penetration while having sex (see Strieber 157). At first, Sarah feels unsettled by the emotions the strange woman evokes in her. She describes her as "[p]erhaps the old definition of a monster, the Latin one" (Strieber 169). The *touch* has worked though. She does not want any intimacy with Tom and feels compelled to be nasty to him (see Strieber 165). Yet, Sarah's feelings are confused at first. She senses that Miriam is lonely and pities her for it. She also finds her beautiful. Yet, she senses that the woman is dangerous: "the woman—thing—[is] frightening and dangerously seductive. She [has] the power to call up desires best left sleeping. Sarah want[s] no part of her" (Strieber 199). When she awakes in Miriam's house after having been drugged by her and transfused with her blood, she allows the other woman to wash her:

> Miriam first massage[s] her neck and shoulders and then washe[s] her back and buttocks with mountains of heady lather. The delicately bristled brush tickle[s] delightfully. It [is] most relaxing. She [doesn't] stir as Miriam [does] her thighs and calves, then sluice[s] her with water. There [comes] a gentle tug at her shoulder and Sarah turn[s] around. She let[s] Miriam bathe her, feeling a little embarrassed more than a little touched. (Strieber 212)

Only when she is back in the laboratory, does Sarah feel agitated about what has passed between her and Miriam (see Strieber 215). But when Miriam returns to the lab to allow Sarah and her fellow scientists to study her, Sarah feels the need to protect her. Even while being examined in the clinic, Miriam lures the other woman: "All through the skull series Sarah let[s] Miriam stare into her eyes. It [is] a wonderful, mesmerizing experience, like being naked before one you truly loved" (Strieber 278). Although Sarah has found out about Miriam's blood in her own system, she still feels fascinated by the other woman: "Miriam was so very beguiling, as mysterious and beautiful as a jewel" (283). Sarah even defends Miriam's deed and blames her alien mind for the act (see Strieber 292). What may have been left of her resistance and caution is broken, however, once Sarah has taken blood from a human offered to her by Miriam. When Tom comes to Miriam's house to rescue Sarah, she lets him make love to her. Yet, she notices that her feelings for him have changed. "She love[s] him [...] as she might love a child. His sexual significance, in the past few days, [have] dwindled to nothing" (Strieber 338). In the end, Sarah cannot help but give in to Miriam's seduction, thereby threatening the sexual status quo (see Palmer 159). Miriam's manipulation even leads to Sarah killing her former lover (see Strieber 340).

5.2.3. The Female Vampire Plays With Human Beings

Miriam's search for eternal love has been explained with her loneliness. While she certainly thinks she loves her companions, her relationship with them resembles that of a pet owner with his animal companion: "human beings [give] her the love that pets give. She [seeks] companionship, some warmth, the appearance of home. [...] After all, [does] she not also deserve some love?" (Strieber 94). She keeps them like toys or slaves, yet her ability to *touch* them makes them forget about the manipulation, at least for a while. Also, the way she picks her human companions reminds of slave owners buying their slaves. They have to be strong like Eumenes, and they have to show determination, arrogance, intelligence and the mind of a predator (see Strieber 103). When Eumenes is successfully turned, she almost treats him like a doll: "she clothe[s] [him] in the finest silks, like a Babylonian prince. She dresse[s] his hair with unguents and applie[s] ocher to his eyes" (Strieber 36). Her companions are supposed to be perfect (see Strieber 47). It is Lollia's beauty that makes Miriam choose her as her lover after Eumenes' body has started to age. In John she admires his youth and freshness (see Strieber 19). Yet, when she finds out about his ageing, she has already decided for her thirteen year old neighbour Alice to be his successor. The girl is chosen because of "her sullen intelligence, her youth and haunting beauty" (Strieber 67). With Dr. Sarah's help, she wants to make Alice immortal like herself. Sarah's knowledge and expertise shall prevent Alice from ever starting to age. Not only do Miriam's lovers not have a choice in the life changing decision she makes for them, her telepathic manipulation also leads to them being dependent on her: "Miriam look[s] forward to the time when Alice would want only her, care only about her, live for their life together" (72). Miriam does not even reconsider her choice of Alice when the girl innocently tells her that she does not find the thought of immortality alluring (see Strieber 68). Miriam spends a lot of time with the girl and she feels that "[t]he girl [is] coming along well" (Strieber 20). Even though Miriam does have feelings for her companions, she thinks about them as one would about objects not human beings. Miriam also feels possessive towards Alice. When the girl is killed by John, Miriam is furious: "How dare he take Alice. She belong[s] to Miriam, not to him" (142). After the girl's death, Sarah becomes Miriam's new project: "Before, Sarah Roberts would have been used and discarded. Now she would be kept" (161). She plans her approach of the doctor carefully and justifies her interference with Sarah's life as "bring[ing] Sarah the gift she most crave[s]: the opportunity to fill that void" in her heart (163). Even when Miriam notices that the scientist does not give in to her easily, she continues to play games with her. She seemingly agrees to the Sarah's and her colleagues' scheme and lets them lock her into the psychiatric ward. All this time she counts on Sarah's loyalty towards her, a feeling that is only evoked in Sarah because of the *touch* she has exercised on her (see Strieber 284). When Sarah already knows what is happening to her body and that life as she has known it is over, Miriam still allows her to go home to see Tom. Miriam knows that as a newly turned vampire Sarah will crave blood and hopes for the woman to attack her lover. Yet, Sarah proves to be stronger, she even sees through Miriam's plan (see Strieber 322, 326). Miriam also uses Tom as a piece in her game. She orchestrates the people around her like a master of puppets does his puppets. Miriam knows that John has freed the creatures in the boxes in the attic. He intends for them to attack Miriam and kill her. When Tom comes to her house to rescue Sarah, Miriam plans to combine both events to her advantage. She lets the remnants of her former companions assail Tom but they are too weak to harm him. Sarah decides against the fate Miriam has chosen for her and attempts to commit suicide in order to remain a human being. But it only leads her to the horrible existence Miriam's former lovers have to endure. Again, the vampire has a casket at hand and another love of her life to keep in the attic. And Miriam will not stop playing her games and keeping her lovers close by like memorabilia of past times.

5.2.4. Miriam Blaylock as a Threat to Those Who Wish to be Immortal and Those Who Do Not Have a Choice

Life changes drastically for those who fall prey to Miriam's promise of immortality. The transformation takes time while the vampire transfuses her own blood into her future companions' bodies. Often, their bodies react to the alien substance with a fever that almost kills them. When they survive, they awake with a hunger unknown to them before. Their body craves sustenance in the form of blood and, having been human before, they have to get used, firstly, to the new diet, and secondly, to the killing of human beings it involves. Their morals are questioned but all, except for Sarah, accept their fate and, guided by Miriam, give in to their new life. She defends the need to kill: "'All you've done is trade one way of life for another. [...] You've joined a new race. We have our rights too. And we never kill more than we need [...] You're more than human now. You've acquired the right of life and death over human beings'" (Strieber 342). What makes Miriam's withholding of the whole truth even worse is that she does so on purpose. She lures them with the promise of eternal life and hides the full truth until her companions cannot turn back (see Strieber 71). Then, Miriam convinces them of the beauty of being like her. In her point of view, they only have to "discover their true lust for existence" (Strieber 71). Once again, she justifies the terrible wrongs she inflicts on them. Miriam's promise of eternal life and love not only means merely delaying ageing for her chosen companions but also existence in a state between life and death once their youth starts to evaporate. They are caught in a state of perpetual hunger which they are no more able to satisfy. Eumenes is reduced to being "a shriveled thing [...] unrecognizable as Eumenes" (91). His digestive system is no longer capable of taking in blood (see Strieber 91). With the loss of the necessary and revitalising Sleep, John's body undergoes the same horrible transformations. It starts with his beard growing again for the first time in almost two hundred years (see Strieber 43). At first he can delay the ageing process temporarily by drinking blood, yet his sudden craving is insatiable. His body becomes older and weaker and his emotions change between aggression to self pity to exhilaration. In the end, he, like those before him, is reduced to being a mere hissing shape, too weak to feed, unable to die a final death and confined into a coffin-like casket for the rest of time. His destiny is outlined by Strieber with the depiction of Methusela's dying. The ape, Sarah's project for the past five years, suddenly stops sleeping, consequently becomes extremely aggressive and even kills another rhesus. Finally, after only a couple of hours, he perishes. Even his body decays rapidly until there only remains a pile of dust (see Strieber 74-5). Miriam's lovers are not granted a final death. Their end is undignified and horrible. Yet, in a twisted sense of morality, Miriam believes that keeping her companions rather than killing them is a kind thing to do (see Pharr 100). She is well aware of the fact that "[f]or love of her [they are] paying an exorbitant price. [They are] losing much more than life, facing an end more terrible than even the worst death" (Strieber 142). Still, out of utter selfishness she keeps betraying them, replacing one with another time after time. "I will keep you beside me for all time until time itself comes to an end. I will neither abandon nor forget you. I will never stop loving you" (319), she whispers to everyone of them, knowing that she has wronged them terribly. Furthermore, she considers her vow of never abandoning them as an admission to betray them (see Strieber 179). Ironically, Miriam cannot imagine being trapped herself. In the clinic, she is terrified by the thought of being restrained and unable to feed (see Strieber162). Yet, she does not grant her lovers final rest but imposes a cruel fate on them. As immortality is atrocious for them, death becomes highly desirable.

6. Jewelle Gomez's *The Gilda Stories*

6.1. *The Vampire in The Gilda Stories*

> You've searched admirably for your humanity.
> Indeed, this is the key to the joy found in our lives,
> maintaining our link in the chain of living things.
> But we are no longer the same as they.
> We are no longer the same as we once were ourselves.
> (Anthony in *The Gilda Stories*, 210)

With *The Gilda Stories*[6] (1991) Jewelle Gomez introduces a black lesbian vampire and her experiences with her extended vampire family. Her story ranges from being a slave in 1850 to being part of an endangered race in an ecologically damaged world in 2050 (see Auerbach 184). Gilda and her companions, vampires of African-American, Creole and Native American descent, share some of the vampiric traits with their predecessors Varney and Lord Ruthven. These are, for instance, immortality, orange gleaming eyes when they are hungry, a sensitivity to the sun, strength and fastness. They do, however, represent good vampires. They abide by certain rules and teach each new vampire to abide by them. The first lesson they are taught is: "Betraying our shared life, our shared humanity makes one unworthy of sharing, unworthy of life." (Gomez 62). By sharing they mean the act of sharing blood. The good vampires in *Gilda* still feed on the blood of humans, they do not, however, kill to do so. Instead, they take only small amounts of blood after having hypnotised the person. Then, they heal the wound and return the gift by implanting a positive dream in the victim's mind. They call this act "the share of the blood" (24). Gilda explains what living like that means to her:

> 'In our life, we who live by sharing the life blood of others have no need to kill. It is through our connection with life, not death, that we live.' [...] "There is a joy to the exchange we make. We draw life into ourselves, yet we give life as well. We give what's needed—energy dreams, ideas. It's a

---

[6] In order to avoid repetition *The Gilda Stories* will be referred to as *Gilda*.

fair exchange in a world full of cheaters. And when we feel it is right, when the need is great on both sides, we can re-create others like ourselves to share life with us. It is not a bad life'. (Gomez 45)

Thus, Gomez does not depict her vampires as bloodthirsty monsters but rather as sympathetic and psychologically complex beings (see Palmer 120). The first Gilda even renounces the traditional vampire lore by telling the Girl: "There are only inadequate words to speak for who we are. The language is crude, the history false. You must look to me and know who I am and if the life I offer is the life you choose. In choosing you must pledge yourself to pursue only life, never bitterness or cruelty" (Gomez 43). In *Gilda*, the act of feeding and blood drinking becomes an "almost sacramental [,] event, instead of a vicious act of survival" (McDonald 175). For Gilda and her fellow vampires, the acquisition of blood means "communion and exchange" (Patterson 47). Furthermore, the vampires in Gilda do not bite their victims but they slice the skin at the neck. After taking their share of the blood, they heal the wound and, unlike other vampires, like for instance Carmilla, they do not have fangs and do not leave any bite marks (see Patterson 47). Thus, many people, no matter of what skin colour, sex, gender or origin, are linked through blood ties without even knowing it. In that sense, *Gilda* is a depiction of "a genuinely multicultural world" (Brinks and Talley 166). Patterson also claims that Gomez feminises "the vampire's masculine power of penetration" (48) by replacing elongated, hard vampire teeth with a "slit reminiscent of a vaginal opening" (48). The feminine aspect is strengthened in that the turning of a vampire is portrayed as a literal birth (see Patterson 48). Before Gilda changes Julius, she kisses his lips "both passionate and chaste, leaving Julius feeling like a child in her arms, yet still a man" (Gomez 192). After she mixes her blood with his by biting her tongue and letting him swallow hers, she "[pulls] her shirt from her chest and [slices] an opening below her breast. She [presses] Julius to her, waiting to feel the power of his mouth taking in the life she [offers]. He [begins] to suck at the blood insistently" (192). After his transformation she tells her vampire friends that "[w]e've finally delivered a brother for me" (Gomez 194; see Patterson 48). In that life-affirming way, vampires do become nurturers and life givers instead of murderers and life takers. Also, Bird, one of Gilda's two creators, tells her that "[the vampires] hunger for connection to life, but it needn't be through horror or destruction" (Gomez 110). There are, however, bad vampires who do enjoy causing death and fear. But they are not part of Gilda's family. Bird makes a clear distinction between vampires like herself and others like Fox, a male vampire pimp who abuses his human prostitutes by saying that "he is not among the living. We are" (Gomez 157). The bad vampires are either killed, like Fox (see Gomez 162), or, like Samuel, they are not allowed membership in the vampire family at the end of the novel when belonging to a community might save the good ones' lives (see Gomez 252). Vampires like Bird and Gilda, then, are no more lethal, but life embracing creatures.

Furthermore, Gilda does not like violence (see Jones 165). Unlike Miriam Blaylock, she only kills when absolutely necessary and when her own life is in danger. This may also be due to the fact that as a human slave, she had watched too many innocent people be attacked and die (see Gomez 180). In fact, she "only" takes the life of three human beings and one other vampire throughout her two hundred year long existence. She commits the first murder as a teenage girl, then named the Girl, before she is turned by killing a man who is about to rape her (see Gomez 11). The feeling of his still warm blood on her skin reminds her of the first bath her mother has given her: "The intimacy of her mother's hands and the warmth of the water lulled the Girl into a trance of sensuality she never forgot. Now the blood washing slowly down her breastbone and soaking into the floor below was like that bath—a cleansing" (Gomez 12). Thus, murder is similar to a purifying act. The Girl's killing of the man who was about to rape her cleanses the world of an evil person and is, therefore, justified.

Another novelty in Gilda is the importance of the vampire family. While Carmilla keeps her family background obscure, and Miriam's primary interest is to find one companion and lover, the vampires in Gilda form social networks (see Palmer 122). And they do so with great care. "[Choosing] someone for [their] family is a great responsibility. It must be done not simply out of [one's] own need or desire but rather because of a mutual need" (Gomez 69). Also, Gilda does not want "to cause such horror" (Gomez 176). Families reshape since the family members do not necessarily have to stay together all their existences long, they may even form other families. Yet, they must not break blood ties (see Gomez 69). That is why Gilda only changes two mortals into vampires. She selects Julius first, but only after careful consideration. He does not have a family anymore and feels not only lonely but also alone as a coloured man amongst whites in New York in the early nineteen seventies. She also gives him a choice by telling him everything there is to know about her family (see Gomez 191). In 2050, Gilda's second choice is a black woman named Ermis, who had planned to commit suicide by taking pills because, like Julius, she has no one left who loves her. That time Gilda does not have the time to consider Ermis as an appropriate member of her family. But after the change the woman lets her know that long life is "the most valuable commodity on the planet" (Gomez 247). They become lovers and Ermis fits into the vampire family perfectly. In the end, Gilda is part of a wonderful family, one she was denied as a mortal because of slavery (see Brinks and Talley 166): "She saw now not just herself but a long line of others who had become part of her as time passed. The family she had hungered for as a child was hers now. It was spread across the globe but was closer to her than she had ever imagined possible" (Gomez 223; see Brinks and Talley 166).

Also, the vampires' home soil is of utmost importance in *Gilda*. The earth of their birthplace as vampires protects them, so they have to sleep in beds in which the soil has been processed into the fabric of the bed (see Gomez 34, 55). Furthermore, their clothes have elements of their native earth woven into it so that they protect the vampires from the sun during the day and even from water (see Gomez 74). By carrying their home soil with them on their extensive travels, the vampires in *Gilda* are rooted creatures nevertheless, since they are always reminded of their origins (see Brinks and Tally 163). On a metaphorical level, Gilda's friendship with the human Savannah is based on their common origin, Mississippi (see Gomez 130-1). It is also the heritage of her Fulani mother that fills Gilda with fond memories of home throughout her life.

Interestingly, vampirism is, unlike in *Carmilla*, not connected to the field of medicine and disease. Instead, it is associated with "the secret religion, vodun" (Gomez 40).

Unlike Carmilla and Miriam, who seduce their human victims, Gilda does not have sexual relationships with hers. On the contrary, Gilda has human friends, she even feels the need to protect humans in danger (see Gomez 156), yet sexual acts only happen with other female vampires. It is only when she has sex that she shares blood with another vampire, first Bird, then Effie and later Ermis, and it is not only a sexual encounter but "functions as a symbolic sexual sharing" (Jones 162):

> [Bird] sliced beneath the right breast and watched, through the thick darkness, the blood which stood even thicker against Gilda's dark skin. She hungrily drew the life through her parted lips into her body.
> This was a desire not unlike their need for the blood, but she had already had her share. It was not unlike lust but less single-minded. She felt the love almost as motherly affection, yet there was more. As the blood flowed from Gilda's body into Bird's they both understood the need—it was for completion. (Gomez 139)

Hence, Gomez separates sex and power, two entities usually combined in vampire lore, in *Gilda*. Consequently, the women concerned are not helpless, unlike, for instance, Laura in *Carmilla* (see Jones 162).

Carmilla takes Laura's blood from her breast. Likewise, Gilda and Bird drink blood from other vampires during the acts of love making or turning a human into a vampire from a cut beneath the other's breast (see Gomez 139, 46).

In *Gilda*, vampires, and not humans, are the endangered ones (see Auerbach 185). In the future, when vampires have been discovered and the world has become a wasteland, they are chased by Hunters, armed humans who enhance their strength and speed by means of drugs. Rich people pay the Hunters for vampire's blood since its transfusion guarantees the recipient humans eternal life. Once humans are transformed into vampires they usually kill their creator (see Gomez 234-5). Like during the times of slavery, Gilda and her family need to hide from their oppressors. The relationship between the hunter and its prey is reformulated (see Jones 165).

Gomez has given her vampires powerful minds. Apart from implanting dreams in a person's consciousness they are able to read other vampires' as well as human beings' minds and are likewise able to speak to them (see Gomez 13). Whenever they choose to they may open up their own minds to others (see Gomez 17, 191) or communicate over large distances with their minds (see Gomez 250). They can also interact with animals in that way (see Gomez 113). The barkeeper at Sorel's bar even uses this ability to "[plant] the seed of forgetfulness" (Gomez 206) in human patrons so that they are not able to deliberately find the bar again. Others like Fox, Savannah and Effie are able to shield their thoughts from others so that they can neither be located nor recognised as vampires (see Gomez 143, 210, 213).

In her work Gomez's vampires are immortal, yet, as Palmer states, they do not necessarily have to stay that way (see Palmer 120). They have the power to end their own lives and the decision is considered to be sacred and has to be respected by the others (see Gomez 50). Vampires find their final death in the ocean. As in *Carmilla*, where Laura's nightly sensations of feeling a rush of water against her breast essentially mean being drained of blood and therefore life by the vampire, water in *Gilda* also has the power to diminish a vampire's power (see Gomez 85), and it can even bring death (see Gomez 48).

6.2. Gilda, the Threat of the Other Reversed

> It had taken many years
> before she was able to distinguish
> between herself and mortals,
> the demarcation still felt fussy at times,
> not quite uncrossable.
> (Gomez 169)

6.2.1. The Black Lesbian Vampire Threatens Male Dominance and the Biased Perception of Women

According to Patterson, Gilda is labelled as Other throughout the novel even before becoming a vampire (see Patterson 36). Her identity is not signified by vampirism alone, but also by her being black and a lesbian. At first, the dominant ones in the novel are the white people, the plantation and therefore slave owners. The Girl only receives the name Gilda after she is turned into a vampire. She meets her name giver Gilda[7] and the other women at a brothel, Woodard's, and apart from her and Bird, Gilda's girlfriend and a vampire of Native American descent, only the cook is coloured. The other women are white. Yet, although she seems like an outsider in that particular community, Gomez writes her "in" (see Hall 395). The events are told from her point of view, depicting the communions she is *not* part of as Other and outside her realm. Gomez also reverses Otherness by making her protagonist a lesbian vampire of colour, whose experiences cast white men as Other (see Patterson 37). At the beginning of the novel the Girl remembers her mother describing white people as "just barely human. Maybe not even. They suck up the world, don't taste it" (Gomez 11, see Patterson 37). That way, features that are usually attributed to vampires are ascribed to white people. Thereby, they are labelled as Other. Similarly, the traditional depiction of vampires who ruthlessly take blood from their victims is inverted when the Girl flees from the plantation and is almost raped by a white man. Her body becomes a commodity in a double sense. Firstly, she is a black slave and therefore owned by the plantation owner and

---

[7] The first Gilda is a white vampire who chooses the Girl to join her vampire family. Together with Bird she turns the Girl and then chooses to die a final death.

secondly, a man tries to dominate and own her body as a woman. Again, she recalls stories her mother used to tell her about their native country Africa, and the Girl describes the offender as "the beast from this *other* land" (Gomez 11, see Patterson 37, emphasis added by Patterson). Hence, Gomez turns the American man into an invader even though the event takes place in the United States, to be precise in Louisiana. Before he is able to penetrate the Girl, "she enter[s] him with her heart which [is] now a wood-handled knife. [...] Warmth spread[s] from his center of power to his chest as the blood [leaves] his body" (Gomez 11, see Patterson 37). Patterson understands the expression "the center of power" as phallic and associates it with "aggressive male sexuality" (Patterson 37). As before, the Girl reverses the threat of male dominance and aggression by taking control of the situation and killing the man herself. She does not become the victim of the vampiric white man and stays in control over her own body (see Patterson 37). Not only is the Girl presented as a strong and powerful woman in the novel, but men are also referred to as animals by her (see Hall 410): "'On the road I met many more beasts on two legs than on four. My fears were not of wolves or mountain cats. They have an understanding of the reasoning of nature. I found it comforting to share that reasoning that needs no words. But with men there is no reasoning at all sometimes.'" (Gomez 67; see Hall 410). Gomez refers to the notion of man as the rational gender. At the same time that rationality is questioned by Gilda's remark about men's violence on the road (see Hall 410).

The Victorian attribution of women to the private sphere and men to the public sphere is again of significance in *Gilda*. Gilda refuses to subject to the norms of the time and dresses as a man. That way she is able to "travel unmolested" (Gomez 66) and roam the streets at night in search of someone to share the blood. She explains her cross-dressing to Anthony, a homosexual vampire who she meets in Yerba Buena, that is San Francisco's old name:

> I realized before I left home there would be no place for me on the road, alone. Even with my advantages I'd be fair game for every male passerby. It seemed easier to simply keep to myself and let people make

> presumptions. A funny thing though ... [...] at least four times—four times—on the road [...] I met others just like me. I mean women dressed like boys. Just going around from place to place trying to live free. (Gomez 66)

Like with slavery, which the Girl evaded by fleeing the plantation, Gilda defies social rules as restriction and uses the prevailing presumptions of her time to her advantage. Due to her disguise she is regarded as a strong man and not as a weak woman. She even gains enough confidence and stops hiding both her sex and her gender. "Gilda [strolls] casually, ignoring the fact that she [is] one of the few women on the street. The men who [move] around her [look] curious but [say] nothing. They [are] startled by her dark skin and the force of her stride" (Gomez 91; see Patterson 46). Moreover, as a vampire and a predator, Gilda is the one who hunts other people, no matter whether they are men are women (see Patterson 46).

In 1890, when the female vampire Eleanor takes her to a tailor to have her try a new appropriate wardrobe, she decides to wear pants instead of dresses, although she knows that this will cast her as an outsider (see Gomez 72). She figures that she need not meet society's demands since "[m]ost would only see her as a former slave" anyhow (Gomez 72). Even later, in 1921, she "[longs] to be free of the dress and stockings, to wear her dark, men's trousers and woolen shirt" (109).

The fact that Gilda does not like to behave conforming to social and moral standards also becomes apparent in a conversation she has with Houston, one of the guards she pays to protect her from the Hunters in 2050, and he alludes to the Victorian notion of women being delicate and weak[8].

(see Hall 399):

---

[8] This concept is discussed in greater detail in chapter 2.2.

'I'm sorry Houston, you startled me.'
'I thought you were fainting.'
'We don't faint, Houston.'
'All women faint,' he [says], chuckling.
'No, Houston, all women do not faint. They haven't in some time.'
(Gomez 240)

It is not only the notion of woman that Gomez questions but also the concept of family. According to Hall, in *Gilda* the individual characters, both female and male, can choose and create their family (see Hall 401). This means that the gendered norms of the necessity of a male and a female agent for the creation of a family is evaded. Furthermore, the importance of heterosexuality in that matter and even the procreating act itself is scrutinised. Gilda chooses adults as members of her family, not children. Not only the transformation of a human into a vampire, but also the sharing of blood between two vampires, is depicted as a birth. Sexual desire intermingles with love between lover, mother and child (see Hall 401):

> Bird pulled Gilda across her chest and sliced the skin beneath her own breast. She pressed Gilda's mouth to the red slash, letting the blood wash across Gilda's face. Soon Gilda drank eagerly, filling herself, and as she did her hand massaged Bird's breast, first touching the nipple gently with curiosity, then roughly. She wanted to know this body that have her life. Her hear swelled with their blood, a tide between two shores. To an outsider the sight may heave been one of horror: their faces red and shining, their eyes unfocused and black, the sound of their bodies slick with wetness, tight with life. Yet it was a birth. The mother finally able to bring her child into the world, to look at her. It was not death that claimed Gilda. It was Bird. [...] She lingered over her as she would a child. She whispered sweet words to her as she might a lover.
> (Gomez 140)

Another inequality that Gilda reverses is, as Patterson claims, that of slave and plantation owner (see Patterson 47). One night, while she is out searching for someone to feed on, she encounters two men on horse, who, equipped with a whip, want to teach her as "one more niggah a lesson" (Gomez 113). But she does not submit to the power structure the men have been used to and breaks one of the attackers' neck and teaches the other one a lesson of her own. "She [cracks] the whip once over his head, then [lays] a stroke across his back"

(113). Then she observes that the shock of the role reversal "[seems] to startle him more than the pain" (113). Again, it is her vampirism that provides her with the strength to attack and severely hurt or kill two men respectively. But above all it is "her repeated and successful refusal to be a victim" (Patterson 47) as well as her strength and the ability to defend herself (see Hall 398) that pose a threat to the established dominant members of society.

6.2.2.   Race as a Question of Otherness

It has been mentioned before that *Gilda* centralises a black vampire instead of focusing on a white protagonist. From the very beginning of the novel the Girl, and later the transformed vampire Gilda, is aware of her being Other due to her race and ethnicity. Having fled from the plantation, she often remembers her childhood on the plantation and the stories her mother told her about Africa. The brothel to her is "this white world" (Gomez 17), and she does not "know where she fit[s] in" (19) with the white women working there. It is "the African face" (30) of her mother that comforts her in situations like these. The Girl is not the only person of colour at Woodard's. "Many [men] [come] just to see [Bird]" (14), a Lakota Indian, who is "ranked among the local curiosities" (14). Both Bird and the Girl know and accept that they are Other than the dominant white culture (see Patterson 39). When Bird decides to teach the Girl how to read, the latter does not understand why she should do so since "[n]o one she knew ever had need of reading, except the black preacher who came over on Saturday nights to deliver a sermon [...]" (Gomez 20). Bird notices that the Girl does not relate to what the Girl perceives as "this new world" (21) when "[she] gazed into the African eyes which struggled to see a white world through words on a page. Bird wondered what creatures, as invisible as she and the Girl were, did with their pasts" (Gomez 21; see Patterson 39). Both women also become invisible when they spend an afternoon in New Orleans. The Girl notices how "creamy-colored quadroons" (Gomez 28) ignore them and "tried to look through Bird as if she were glass and simply dismissed her as a slave" (28). It is important to note that the Girl is ashamed in front of those women. She experiences discrimination by people who "[share] her African blood" (28). Gilda is aware of the fact that her skin colour does not grant her and Bird a place in a society which oppresses dark skinned people and favours fair skinned ones. Only later, when she has been turned into a vampire and has taken her name, does she overcome the social boundaries binding her because of her skin colour (see Patterson 39). It is then that she becomes proud of herself and her skin colour and withstands society's privilege of fair skin. When she looks at her image in the mirror and regards her hair, "[t]he kinkiness of it reassured her" (Gomez 56; see Patterson 40). Her pride can also be seen when she "marvel[s] at her body's fineness. Her brown skin shone like a polished stone; the rounded stomach and full legs were unchanged from those of her ancestors" (Gomez 197; see Patterson 40).

Also, she thinks of the city she is staying in at that time, Yerba Buena, as home. It is also home "to those like herself" (Gomez 56). The fact that this phrase can either refer to people of dark skin or to vampires alike illustrates that she does not define herself as Other only by the colour of her skin but also by being a vampire. This does not, however, mean that her racial heritage is not of utmost importance to her. On the contrary, the vampire never forgets what being a black woman means:

> The inattention of her contemporaries to some mortal questions, like race, didn't suit her. She didn't believe a past could, or should, be so easily discarded. Her connection to the daylight world came from her blackness. The memories of her master's lash as well as her mother's face, legends of the Middle Passage, lynchings she had not been able to prevent, images of black women bent over scouring brushes—all fueled her ambition. (Gomez 180)

This means, as Patterson states, that Gilda does not favour being a vampire over being black. She refuses to forget about her personal as well as ethnic history (see Patterson 41).

6.2.3. Heterosexuality Scrutinised

It is important to note that Gomez attaches more value to homosexuality in *Gilda* than to heterosexuality, not only for the female but also for the male characters (see Patterson 45). Gilda witnesses relationships between both homosexuals and heterosexuals, and it is the former that show an equality between both partners. The first relationship the Girl observes is that between the first Gilda and Bird. Although she has heard people whisper about them being different due to their secret religion, she is not afraid of "these two who [sleep] so soundly in each other's arms and [treat] her with such tenderness" (Gomez 40). One day the Girl overhears them arguing. Yet, they reconcile shortly afterwards knowing that they fight "only because [they] love each other" (40). Also, the relationship between Sorel and Anthony is based on love and respect for each other. Gilda moans about Bird having left her to travel the world. Anthony, however, has nothing but understanding for Sorel, who has left for New Zealand with Bird to right some wrongs among landowners (see Gomez 175). In 1921, when Gilda lives on a farm in Missouri, she meets Aurelia, a black human widow. They become friends and plan on building schools for poor people. Gilda's feelings for the other woman grow and she wonders whether Aurelia "might be suited to this life, or [whether] she might simply be thinking of her own desire and not the needs of others" (Gomez 119). Aurelia also has feelings for Gilda, yet the vampire decides against turning the other woman. Aurelia has numerous dreams and ideas about how to help other people. Gilda feels that it is these dreams "that [hold] Aurelia to the earth" (124). A life without the other woman is best for both of them, that is why Gilda leaves. At that time she has not seen Bird for over hundred years. Still, she is an "ancient reality" (136) to Gilda, and not one day has passed without Gilda thinking about her. All this time they have stayed in contact through communicating in their minds (see Gomez 136). When they meet again in the mid 1950s, there is, however, a void between them. Bird envies Gilda's connection with Savannah (see Gomez 154). Yet, they still love each other, and there is no question of Bird helping Gilda fight Fox. Moreover, Bird has accepted that Gilda has not been responsible for her namegiver's final death.

She has learned that the first Gilda chose to die of her own will (see Gomez 140-1). There is no power struggle between the first Gilda and Bird, nor between Anthony and Sorel or Gilda and Effie. Even during the act of making love submission of one partner is not exploited by the other. Instead, the submissive person experiences power and pleasure at the same time (see Hall 415):

> Effie's mouth and hands were tender, insistent—demanding Gilda's pleasure be allowed its own way. Gilda enjoyed the sensation of yielding. [...] When she felt the welling of heat inside her she knew the release would be greater than any she had known before and she opened her eyes to catch Effie's gaze. [...] At the final moment Gilda closed her eyes, inside herself as the power of her desire erupted around them. (Gomez 213)

The only homosexual bonding that is portrayed in a negative light is that between Gilda and Eleanor. Gilda feels attracted to the other vampire, yet she has to learn that Effie is manipulative. She uses other people for her own advantage. One day, when the two of them are together, they are interrupted by Samuel, who tries to kill Gilda. Instead of supporting Gilda, Eleanor stays away from the fight and only tells the other woman to kill the attacker. It is then that Gilda realizes that she does not want to act or even less kill on another person's command, and she tells Eleanor: "No, Eleanor, I can't kill him for you. [...] I'm no longer a servant, Miss Eleanor. We been freed" (Gomez 99).

Platonic homosocial relationships are also privileged. When in New York in 1971 Gilda has a circle of mortal friends, all of whom are women, some of whom are lesbians. Their friendship and relations are depicted in a positive light. The relationship between Savannah and Skip, two mortals, is depicted as close and caring. That is why he does not hesitate to help her, Gilda and Bird to fight Fox. He even brings her favourite pillow to the house they plan to overpower the pimp at (see Gomez 150). Yet, Savannah mistrusts him when she finds out that there is a stash of heroin in the attic (see Gomez 159).

There is a constant struggle between Fox and Toya. This may be due to the fact that he is a pimp and she works for him as a prostitute. Yet, their work relationship does not entitle him to treat her without respect or dignity. The same behaviour is true for those two men who tried to hurt Gilda with their whip (cf. chapter 5.2.1.). Their treatment of women and black people is derogatory and violent. Likewise, Samuel, a white heterosexual vampire, is a cruel character who wishes to manipulate Gilda and others. He is described by Anthony as possessing "no real understanding of our world" (Gomez 208; see Patterson 49). Interestingly, Samuel and Fox, both heterosexual vampires, represent the bad vampires in *Gilda* (see Brinks and Talley 164).

The only heterosexual man who does not exert any power over women is Julius, a young black man, who Gilda also meets in New York and whom she transforms into a vampire in the course of time (see Gomez 191). Although he is interested in Gilda at first and asks her out several times, she only loves him like a brother. He does not want to lose her as a friend and accepts her offer of friendship and family when she shows him what her world is like before she turns him (see Gomez 191).

6.2.4.   Gilda as a Threat to the Self-Perception of Humanity

Gilda is a story that depicts the journey of a female vampire's journey through time and space. In her bicentennial existence Gilda witnesses and experiences social grievances such as slavery, racism and the exclusion of minorities like prostitutes. Although some of these take place within her vampiric world, it is the human world they are all part of. The members of Gilda's vampire family live among humans, yet as time passes, they interact with them less and less. At the end of the nineteenth century, humans and vampires intermingled at Sorel's bar in Yerba Buena (see Gomez 59). By 1981, when he owns a club in New York, humans are tricked out of the bar with the help of the barkeeper's mind (see Gomez 207). Gilda does have human friends, like Ayeesha and the group of girls around her, and Savannah, she does however understand that a certain distance between herself and the others is necessary (see Gomez 200). Her understanding, though, is the product of a long learning process. For a long time Gilda could not differentiate between mortals and those like herself (see Gomez 169). Yet, over time, she has come to realize that they are not alike and that sharing her life with them is problematic. Gomez's vision of the future depicts humanity on the verge of decay, not only ecologically, but also socially. In 2020, race and skin colour still seem to divide people as they "[try] to decide if brown people and white people should eat sitting at the same table" (Gomez 225). By 2050, the moon can only be seen when "the night breeze [blows] the heavy chemical clouds away". And people have to pass a health test in order to be allowed to live in the "Off-world" they have inhabited because they have polluted the earth irreversibly. Existence has become a matter of life and death, not only for humans, but also for vampires. Yet, despite all the adversities, mortals desire longevity and chase vampires for their blood to prolong their own lives. They have become morally corrupt. The vampires, on the other hand, remain close and cherish their family bond. Patterson states that *Gilda* implies that the vampires will be the ones "to survive and grow beyond and in spite of [the dominant culture of humans]—*not* with it" (50). While humanity is doomed to perish, the former monster at the margins will thrive and live on.

7. Further Threats: the Uncanny and the Abject in *Carmilla, The Hunger* and *The Gilda Stories*

7.1. Carmilla, The Gilda Stories, The Hunger *and The Uncanny*

> There was also this feeling,
> strange and yet remembered.
> (*The Hunger* 8)

Sigmund Freud defines his concept of the uncanny as "that species of the frightening that goes back to what was once well known and had long been familiar" (124). The German word *heimlich* (familiar) merges with its antonym *unheimlich* (unfamiliar), thus what is called *heimlich* becomes *unheimlich*. The word *heimlich*, Freud continues, can mean two different things: on the one hand, it describes what is comfortable and familiar, and on the other hand, it relates to what is kept hidden and concealed (see Freud 132). Laura's father is English and the two of them speak English albeit living in Austria "partly to prevent its becoming a lost language among [them], and partly from patriotic motives" (Le Fanu 73). Since her father is the only parent left, their English patriotism may be the reason why Laura does not feel at home in Styria. The core of the word *heimlich, Heim*, means home in English. This means that instead of feeling *heim-lich*, i.e. at home in Austria, she feels *un-heim-lich*, not at home, a foreigner - uncanny. Similarly, Gilda cannot forget her Fulani heritage. Although she herself was born in Louisiana, it is her mother's African origin that Gilda associates with home. She constantly searches for a place to belong to, yet she feels as an outsider among the predominantly white girls at Woodard's. When she is turned into a vampire, she finds a family she feels at home with.

Freud then analyses situations and things that people find uncanny and refers to Ernst Jentsch's case of "doubt as to whether an apparently animate object really is alive and, conversely, whether a lifeless object might not perhaps be animate" (Jentsch qtd. in Freud 135). As an example Jentsch mentions the effect brought about by wax figures. Yet, vampires can arouse the same uncanny feelings in humans as beings that are neither dead nor alive. Like a corpse Carmilla rests in a coffin during the night to regain strength (see Le Fanu 134). At the same time, Laura says that the vampire's "features [...] were tinted with the warmth of life" (Le Fanu 134). Similarly, the test results in Sarah's laboratory show that Miriam is alive. Yet, her brain is like that of a dead person (see Strieber 174).

In an analysis of E. T. A. Hoffmann's *The Elixirs of the Devil*, Freud mentions other motifs that evoke an uncanny effect in the reader. One is the theme of the *Doppelgänger*, i.e. a person who looks like another, a double. This is what Miriam intends to make of Sarah, she wants her "to become an equal in every sense of the word" (Strieber 344). In a wider sense, this is also what happens to Miriam's companions. Once their ageing cannot be stopped, they become shadows of their former selves, resembling barely alive corpses. They symbolise another uncanny factor, that of "the repetition of the same thing" (Freud 143). Although Miriam has experienced several times what a dreadful fate her companions have to meet, she does not stop creating a new companion every time her current one starts to age. According to Freud, the uncanny feeling is deepened by "spontaneous transmission of mental processes from one of these persons to the other [...] so that the one becomes co-owner of the other's knowledge, emotions and experience" (141-2). This is exactly what happens in *The Hunger* and *Gilda*. Miriam is able to share emotions with other people by means of a *touch*. Moreover, she also has the power to implant certain thoughts in the other persons' mind without their consent. Hence, an uncanny effect is produced when she evokes homosexual desires in Sarah while she is sleeping. The effect is even intensified when Sarah, who was suspicious of her own feelings at first, rejects her boyfriend and feels attracted towards Miriam. And Gilda can open her mind to others and let them see and feel what she sees and experiences.

Freud further states that the uncanny is also "represented by anything to do with death, dead bodies, revenants, spirits and ghosts" (148). This has to do with humanity's notion of death. Death and mortality are concepts the human mind cannot grasp consciously; therefore, they evoke uncanny feelings. Yet, Freud further claims that "[t]he false semblance of death and the raising of the dead" do not represent uncanny themes since "they are commonplace in fairy tales" (153). Hence, the very nature of Carmilla's, Miriam's and Gilda's existence as vampires, then, does not make them uncanny. But the fact that all of them have tricked mortality does. Carmilla "was all but assassinated in [her] bed" (Le Fanu 101). The act left her changed forever and she became immortal, captured in her youth for all times. Gilda equally escapes death when Bird completes the circle the first Gilda started in the turning of the Girl (see Gomez 46-8). Like Carmilla, she remains young forever as long as she satisfies her body's need for blood. As for Miriam, it is not clear how she became the creature she is. Yet, it is known that she belongs to an alien species, which constitutes a similar type of uncanniness.

Freud then continues that "an uncanny effect often arises when the boundary between fantasy and reality is blurred, when we are faced with the reality of something that we have until now considered imaginary [...]" (150). This is certainly true for all the people in the novels discussed who find out that vampires do indeed exist and that they even live among humans. Sarah experiences uncanniness when she finds out that mortality can indeed be conquered. She works on an experiment with monkeys that might hold the key to immortality. As a scientist Sarah is used to finding rational explanations for scientific problems. Thus, when the tests carried out on Miriam reveal that the latter is not part of the human species, the stability of Sarah's reality collapses and produces an uncanny effect. It is even deepened when Sarah finds out that Miriam has transfused her own blood into Sarah's body. The alien blood cells will dominate Sarah's and, as a consequence, she will change into a member of the race Miriam is part of.

So far, the uncanny has been discussed in relation to beliefs that were once considered to be true. In the course of time they have been "surmounted"

(Freud 154) and declared untrue. Thus, an uncanny feeling arises when these old thoughts do indeed come true and are confirmed. They become a "question of material reality" (154).

A different kind of uncanniness is evoked when something that is known from experience is revived: "the uncanny [...] is something familar [sic!] [...] that has been repressed and then reappears [...]" (Freud 152). At the same time Freud argues that not all repressed desires or memories that remind us of them are uncanny. It depends on the circumstances in which the repressed reappears (see Freud 152-153). As for repressed childhood complexes, Freud concludes that "the uncanny element we know from experience arises either when repressed childhood complexes are revived by some impression, or when primitive beliefs that have been *surmounted* appear to be once again confirmed" (155). This is also true for *Carmilla*. When Carmilla first visits Laura when the latter is about six years old, she wakes up during the night and sees a young lady in the room. She falls asleep with the lady caressing her soothingly and wakes up because she experiences a pain in her breast caused by what felt like two needles (see Le Fanu 74). Her father, as well as the governesses, assure her that her experience was only a dream. Even at the age of twenty-seven, when Laura recounts her story to Dr. Hesselius' assistant, she remembers that the incident "produced a terrible impression upon [her] mind, which, in fact, never has been effaced" (Le Fanu 74). When Carmilla enters Laura's world again, when she is nineteen years old, she is presented as a real breathing being, and Laura recognises her. This, however, has an uncanny effect; it frightens Laura and "produce[s] a terrible impression upon [her] mind" (75), for up to the moment of recognition, she had thought about the young lady as a product of her own fantasy. The effect is repeated when Carmilla also acknowledges Laura with a "strange fixed smile of recognition" (85) from a similar dream she herself had twelve years ago. And although the situation seems *unheimlich* to Laura, the feeling of recognition makes the strange girl *heimlich* to her at the same time (see Waltje 43 ff.).

Another incident of the theme of recognition-without knowing occurs when Laura once more dreams of an intruder during the night. That time she sees a large, black cat-like creature in her room and subsequently experiences the same sensation of two needles darting into her breast. Again, Carmilla also confesses having had the same nightmare the same night, yet the figure in her room disappeared the moment she touched a charm against the oupire. Looking back as a grown-up to the events of her adolescence, Laura does not understand "how [she] overcame [her] horror so effectually [...]" (Le Fanu 104). The theme discussed is reversed when Laura and her father meet General Spielsdorf, who they know but hardly recognise due to his altered appearance (see Le Fanu 115). His account, however, produces an uncanny effect in so far as it is very similar to what Laura and her father had gone through themselves. He tells them that he met a woman and her daughter at a masked ball, and the mother had to go on an urgent trip to a foreign country, where she could not take her daughter with her. In listening to his description, Laura and her father are able to recognise their own experiences from a distance. The General's story is a little different, though, since the woman claims that they know each other, yet she does not take off her mask. This means that the woman, in contrast to Carmilla, is known but not recognised (see Gelder 45). Upon her reminder, incidents are evoked in his mind "that instantly started into life at her touch" (Le Fanu 119). The General's narrative evokes another uncanny effect when he mentions the name of the woman's daughter, Millarca. Like Mircalla, it is an anagram of Carmilla's name. His wife was a descendant of the Countess of Karnstein, as was Laura's mother. When Laura first meets Carmilla in her dream the latter resembles a young woman. She could be seen as the mother the girl lost at a young age. She had repressed memories of her, and at that moment her fear evoked her image as a young and beautiful woman. Thus, an uncanny effect is created. Also, the restored picture of Mircalla, Countess Karnstein, bears an uncanny resemblance to Carmilla. This effect is revoked when Laura finds out that the woman in the picture is indeed Carmilla.

7.2. Carmilla, The Gilda Stories, The Hunger *and The Abject*

> So this was Miriam's "food".
> Sarah gagged with the memory of it.
> And yet it sang in her veins.
> Slowly she extended her hand.
> Her own eyes closing as if she were
> under the influence of some opiate,
> she stroked the forehead of the person
> whose life she had taken.
> (*The Hunger* 318)

In her book *The Powers of Horror* Kristeva explores the concept of the abject. It refers to the pre-lingual reaction of a human being, expressed through the body through, for instance, vomiting or nausea, to the lack of distinction between "I" and and "other" (3). Abjection can be caused by various things, among them the corpse, food loathing or an open wound (see Kristeva 3). According to Kristeva, "[a]bjection preserves what existed in the archaism of pre-objectal relationship, in the immemorial violence with which a body becomes separated from another body in order to be [...]" (10). This means that Kristeva's theory deals with how a human being, more precisely, a baby, develops a sense of 'I' as a subject opposed to others as objects. Before that happens, Kristeva mentions the Platonic concept of 'chora', a space in which the not yet speaking human does not yet know about "the prohibition placed on the maternal body" (14). The baby, therefore, does not acknowledge any boundaries between itself and the maternal body. It is subject to "drives, whether life drives or death drives" (14). A human being experiences abjection for the first time when it is separated from the mother's body. In the act of breaking away from the other body, the child becomes itself. In doing so, however, the mother turns into the abject and is repelled and rejected (see Kristeva 13). It is the first time when the human being establishes an identity and separates "itself" from "others".

This notion of selfhood and otherhood is important in the reading of *Carmilla* as the selves of Laura and Carmilla are repeatedly merged in the novella (see Lee 30). This starts, as Lee claims, with their shared dreams – as the girls' perspectives merge, so do their characters (see Lee 29). It seems as if Carmilla desires to tear down the boundaries of her self and that of the other, Laura (see Lee 24). Thus, she repeatedly tells Laura: "I live in you" (Le Fanu 98) and Laura "shall die – die, sweetly die – into [her own] life" (89). Interestingly, it is the blood of the Karnstein family, which is essentially Carmilla's blood that runs through Laura's veins. This means that the vampire is right when she tells Laura that she lives in her. At that point of time, the girl, however, is not aware of that fact yet. Laura also does not know that her friend enforces her dying by taking blood from Laura's body, thus taking in Laura's blood and life and at the same time killing the other. This is exactly what Kristeva describes in *The Powers of Horror*: "[The abject] kills in the name of life – a progressive despot; it lives at the behest of death – an operator in genetic experimentations; it curbs the other's suffering for its own profit – a cynic" (15). Carmilla even declares that "you and I are one for ever" (Le Fanu 90), which causes her object of affection to state that she does not know herself when Carmilla talks like that (see Le Fanu 90). Laura is not aware of being related to Carmilla by blood and that as a result, they are one forever. Lee claims that Le Fanu punned this "oneness" when Carmilla talks about seeing Laura in her dream for the first time (see Lee 32): "Your looks *won* me" (Le Fanu 86, my emphasis). Laura then admits that Carmilla won her as well (see Le Fanu 87; see Lee 32). Also, the fact that the same story is provided by two different narrators, Laura and General Spielsdorf, adds to the reader's confusion as to where one self ends and the other begins (see Lee 26).

The same is true for Miriam in *The Hunger*. With her ability to *touch* other people, be it her vampiric creations or humans, she can put images or feelings into their minds. Hence, it is difficult to say which feelings have lain dormant inside the person affected and have been awakened by the *touch* and which are entirely those evoked by Miriam. When she *touches* Sarah, she senses that something is missing in the doctor's life, then she forces images of naked women into her mind. By doing so she enforces her own will on Sarah. By comparison, Gilda and her family give those humans they share the blood with the feelings and dreams the mortal ones need and desire.

There are also some unstable identities in *Gilda*. The Girl becomes Gilda after her name giver has met her final death, and after she has been transformed into a vampire. When Gilda and Bird reunite after a decade and have sex, Bird feels a "motherly affection" (Gomez 139) and Gilda takes blood from a cut beneath Bird's breast. This image brings to mind a child taking its mother's breast. Yet, the act between Gilda and Bird becomes sexual when Gilda massages the other woman's breast (see Gomez 140). Hence, Bird, who has created Gilda as a vampire and therefore is like a mother, feels like a mother - and she consequently becomes abject - and at the same time like a lover for her vampiric daughter, who is also her mistress (see Brinks and Talley 165). Similarly, Gilda feels like a sister towards Julius after she has turned him (see Gomez 194). At the same time she senses "well-being only a child can feel when lying in the arms of its parent" (Gomez 192) from him. Thus, she is his creator, and therefore mother, as well as his sibling. Furthermore, a fusion of selves takes place also in *Gilda*. With the vampires' ability to not only read other peoples' minds but also to plant images into them, the line that separates vampire and "victim" becomes fuzzy (see Brinks and Talley 166).

Kristeva further states that "[t]he corpse, seen without God and outside of science, is the utmost of abjection" (4). She continues that abjection is caused "by what disturbs identity, system and order. What does not respect borders, positions, rules. The in-between, the ambiguous, the composite" (4). This is also true for Carmilla, Gilda and Miriam, given that they are not dead but at the same time not alive like a 'normal' human being. They are in between these states, and this is what goes against order and system. Miriam's very existence as an alien marks a further disruption of order since she has never even been part of the human race. In *Carmilla*, Laura knows the living girl Carmilla; she even recognises it in the vampire Carmilla. But because the latter is not alive and, therefore, technically dead and a corpse, she, like Gilda and Miriam, becomes abject. In that sense Kristeva's concept of the abject is a further development of Freud's uncanny (see Lee 30). Furthermore, Carmilla does not respect the rules concerning moral standards of her time. The same is true for Gilda, who prefers dressing as a man at a time when women were supposed to wear dresses. It has been discussed in chapter 2.2. that homosexuality was considered as an abnormality in the nineteenth century. In that regard, the vampires' homosexuality can also be seen as abject. Hence, Miriam becomes abject in a double sense: firstly, because she is bisexual and secondly, because she seduces Sarah, a woman in a heterosexual relationship. As a result of the manipulation, Sarah is aroused by the thought of naked women and even finds Miriam sexually attractive. Moreover, Miriam cannot keep her promise of immortality, flawlessness and everlasting health. Order is disrupted when her lovers start to age and their existence ends with decay and a perpetual state between life and death (see Creed 68). The fact that she does not grant her former lovers a final death goes against the law of nature. Miriam also shows disrespect to order and rules when she saves Eumenes from death. When Miriam finds him, he has been executed with other members of Spartacus' army and then left to die. Yet, Miriam nurses him back to health, further disrupting the system. Gilda does so similarly with Ermis by transforming the woman who has chosen to end her own life.

Reading *Carmilla, Gilda* and *The Hunger* with regard to abjection, blood also plays an important role. Kristeva states that

> [b]lood, indicating the impure, takes on the "animal" seme of the previous opposition and inherits the propensity for murder of which man must cleanse himself. But blood, as a vital element, also refers to women, fertility, and the assurance of fecundation. It thus becomes [...] the propitious place for abjection where *death* and *femininity, murder* and *procreation, cessation of life* and *vitality* all come together. (96)

Hence, Carmilla and Miriam become abject in two ways. Firstly, they feed on human blood and in order to satiate their thirst, they have to kill their suppliers. Since their existence as a vampire dictates the need for blood and, consequently, the killing of human beings, they can never cleanse themselves of the murders. Secondly, by killing female persons, Carmilla and Miriam take away their inherent ability to reproduce and procreate. Blood, then, is only vital to the vampires, but not for their female victims. For them, blood equals death. Furthermore, Miriam transfuses her own impure blood into Sarah's veins and thereby contaminates her and makes her abject.

Abjection even is part of religion and its practice, be it pagan or monotheistic. The threat of the abject calls for purifying means (see Kristeva 17; see Becker-Leckrone 39). In *Carmilla*, six-year-old Laura is visited by a priest after the vampire's first attack on her. They pray together and often repeat the phrase "Lord, hear all good prayers for us, for Jesus' sake" (Le Fanu 75). She explains that she reiterated these words over and over and even her nurse made her include them in her prayers as an attempt to cleanse her from the threat of the abject. From religion Kristeva draws a line to art, which she calls "catharsis par excellence" (17). By narrating her story to Dr. Hesselius' assistant in order for it to be included in his case studies and therefore be published as a work of art, Laura purifies herself from the abject she has experenced and restores order. Likewise, Gilda writes journals and thereby cleanses herself from the abject (see Gomez 76). Miriam, however, is not cleansed from the abject since she continues to exist.

8. Conclusion

> they all know she's there,
> and no one goes out after dark.
> they tuck their daughters into bed,
> and lock the doors.
> they say, we should have killed her back then,
> when we first knew.
>
> and the daughters lie awake in their beds,
> and smile.
> (Karen Lindsay)

Carmilla, the first literary female vampire with a story of her own, threatens Victorian society because she kills young, innocent girls and by doing so defies male authority. Although she is portrayed as a young girl herself who is in need of a friend, the sympathy the reader feels for her pales considering that her advances always end in death, even though she considers them to be acts of love. Her killing love is not the only risk she poses to nineteenth century moral standards, so is also her sexuality. Laura is attracted to her both emotionally and physically, although she cannot make sense of her sentiments and does not regard them as sexual. However, the fact that she cannot stop thinking about Carmilla even after the latter's final death, that she fancies seeing her shows that there is more to her feelings than friendship only. Since homosexuality was considered to be unnatural at that time, the vampire also presents a danger to the highly valued institution of marriage. This paper has also shown that the characters in the story form a dichotomy, that between women and men. Given that Victorian women were not supposed to express opinions of their own, this is, yet again, a danger to the society of that era. Le Fanu's novella has been influential in that it has challenged and ultimately undermined male authority. Although it is a vampire who is responsible for that, she is a woman nevertheless.

The central story of Miriam Blaylock takes place in the twentieth century, a time when homosexuality was not considered as unnatural. Yet, bisexual Miriam challenges the sexual status quo, since her advances on Sarah, who is in a happy heterosexual relationship, do indeed evoke more than friendly feelings in the latter. The vampire's seduction in Miriam's case end deadly only for those she feeds on. Also, her lovers gain the immortality she promises. Yet, the advantages of longevity dissolve after a couple of centuries when ageing sets in again and reduces her companions to old withering shadows of their former selves, incapable of feeding themselves and, at the same time, unable to die. Miriam's love makes her victims, in this case not the people she feeds on since they find a quick death, hope for an end to their never ending wasting away by being granted a final death. The fact that Miriam believes to act out of love and devotion by keeping her former companions with her in their casket makes her love all the more threatening.

Gilda, a representative of the good vampires, does not need to kill the humans she takes blood from. In fact, she even gives them what they wish for in the form of dreams and hopes. By doing so she shares something positive with them and improves their life, if only for a short time. She does not even take human lovers and that way, unlike Carmilla and Miriam, she does not corrupt heterosexual women for marriage. Hence, Gilda's sexuality does not have an influence on female heterosexuality. She does, however, pose a threat to heterosexuality in general since her story shows that homosexuality is to be favoured over heterosexuality. All the same sex relationships in the novel, both those between vampires and those between humans, are based on equality, respect and love. In contrast, the relationships between partners of the opposite involve power games, inequality and disrespect. In the nineteenth century, Gilda also challenges the social and moral standards of the time, yet not in the same way as Carmilla does. It is not her sexuality that provokes other people's contempt, but it is her refusal to dress and act in a way a woman of that time was supposed to. She prefers to dress as a man because it allows her to move in the world more freely. Yet, women were supposed to stay at home and be doting wives to their husbands and mothers to their children. The novel also depicts the vampires as morally more stable beings than humans. In the future, humans have become corrupt, and everyone just looks after themselves and does not care about other people. The vampires, however, form a unity and look out for each other, and thereby reverse the supposedly position of humanity as the moral and vampires as the immoral species.

9. BIBLIOGRAPHY

9.1 Primary Sources

Gomez, Jewelle. *The Gilda Stories: A Novel*. New York: Firebrand, 1991.
Le Fanu, J. Sheridan. "Carmilla." *The Penguin Book of Vampire Stories*. Ed.
    Alan Ryan. New York: Penguin, 1988. 71-137.
Strieber, Whitley. *The Hunger*. 1991. New York: Pocket, 2001.

9.2 Secondary Sources

Abbott, Stacey. *Celluloid Vampires: Life After Death in the Modern World*.
    Austin: U of Texas P, 2007.
Auerbach, Nina. *Our Vampires, Ourselves*. Chicago: U of Chicago P, 1995.
Becker-Leckrone, Megan. *Julia Kristeva and Literary Theory*. Basingstoke:
    Palgrave Macmillan, 2005.
Beresford, Matthew. *From Demons to Dracula: The Creation of the Modern
    Vampire Myth*. London: Reaktion, 2008.
Brinks, Ellen, and Lee Talley. "Unfamiliar Ties: Lesbian Constructions of Home
    and Family in Jeanette Wintersons's *Oranges Are Not the Only Fruit* and
    Jewelle Gomez's *The Gilda Stories*." *Homemaking: Women Writers and
    the Politics and Poetics of Home*. Ed. Catherine Wiley and Fiona R.
    Barnes. New York: Garland Publishing Inc., 1996. 145-171.
Bristow, Joseph. *Sexuality*. London: Routledge, 1997.
Butler, Judith. "Excerpt from Gender Trouble." *Feminist Social Thought: A
    Reader*. Ed. Tietjens Meyers. London: Routledge, 1997. 112-128.
Byron, Lord George Gordon. "Fragment of a Novel." *The Penguin Book of
    Vampire Stories*. Ed. Alan Ryan. New York: Penguin, 1988. 1-6.
Case, Sue-Ellen. "Tracking the Vampire." *Writing on the Body: Female
    Embodiment and Feminist Theory*. Ed. Katie Conboy, Nadia Medina and
    Sarah Stanbury. New York: Columbia UP, 1997. 380-400.
Christ, Carol. "Victorian Masculinity and the Angel in the House." *A Widening
    Sphere: Changing Roles of Victorian Women*. Ed. Martha Vicinus.
    London: Methuen, 1980. 146-162.
Coleridge, Samuel Taylor. *Christabel*. Oxford: Woodstock, 1991.
Cooper, Sarah. *Relating to Queer Theory: Rereading Sexual Self-Definition
    With Irigaray, Kristeva, Wittig and Cixous*. Bern: Lang, 2000.
Copjec, Joan. "Vampires, Breast-Feeding, and Anxiety." *Gothic: Critical
    Concepts in Literary and Cultural Studies*. Ed. Fred Botting and Dale
    Townshend. London: Routledge, 2004.
Creed, Barbara. *The Monstrous-Feminine: Film, Feminism, Psychoanalysis*.
    London: Routledge, 2005.
Davis, Flora. *Moving the Mountain: The Women's Movement in America Since
    1960*. Champaign: U of Illinois P, 1999.

Day, William Patrick. *Vampire Legends in Contemporary American Culture: What Becomes a Legend Most.* Lexington: UP Kentucky: 2002.

Degele, Nina. *Gender / Queer Studies: Eine Einführung.* Paderborn: Fink, 2008.

Dyer, Richard. "Children of the Night: Vampirism as Homosexuality, Homosexuality as Vampirism." *Sweet Dreams: Sexuality Gender and Popular Fiction.* Ed. Susannah Radstone. London: Lawrence & Wishart Limited, 1988. 47-72.

----. *The Culture of Queers.* London: Routledge, 2002.

Dynes, Wayne R. *Lesbiansm.* New York: Garland, 1992.

Eder, Franz: *Kultur der Begierde: Eine Geschichte der Sexualität.* 2nd ed. München: C.H.Beck, 2009.

Faderman, Lillian. *Surpassing the Love of Men: Romantic Friendship and Love Between Women from the Renaissance to the Present.* London: The Women's Press Limited, 1982.

Farin, Michael. *Heroine des Grauens: Wirken und Leben der Elisabeth Báthory in Briefen, Zeugenaussagen und Phantasiespielen.* München: Kirchheim Verlag, 2003.

Flocke, Petra. *Vampirinnen: "Ich schaue in den Spiegel und sehe nichts": Die kulturellen Inszenierungen der Vampirin.* Tübingen: Konkursbuchverlag Claudia Gehrke, 1999.

Forrest, Katherine. "O Captain, My Captain". *Daughters of Darkness: Lesbian Vampire Tales.* San Francisco: Cleis, 1993. 185-227.

Foucault, Michel. "The History of Sexuality." *Literary Theory.* Ed. Julie Rivkin and Michael Ryan. Malden: Blackwell, 2004. 892-899.

Freud, Sigmund. *The Uncanny.* [*Das Unheimliche*] 1919. Trans. David McLintock. Introd. Hugh Haughton. London: Penguin, 2003.

Frost, Brian J. *The Monster With a Thousand Faces: Guises of the Vampire in Myth and Literature.* Ohio: Bowling Green State U Popular P, 1989.

Gelder, Ken. *Reading the Vampire.* London: Routledge, 1994.

Griffith, Nicola, and Stephen Pagel. *Bending the Landscape: Horror.* New York: The Overlook Press: 2003.

Hall, Lynda. "Passion(ate) Plays 'Wherever We Found Space': Lorde and Gomez Queer(y)ing Boundaries and Acting In." *Callaloo* 23.1 (2000): 394-421.

Hoffmann, Ernst T. A. *Poetische Werke: Die Elexiere des Teufels.* 2 vols. Berlin: de Gruyter, 1958.

Jagose, Annamarie. *Queer Theory: An Introduction.* New York: NY UP, 1996.

Jones, Miriam. "The Gilda Stories: Revealing the Monsters at the Margin." *Blood Read. The Vampire as Metaphor in Contemporary Culture.* Ed. Joan Gordon and Veronica Hollinger. Philadelphia: U of Pennsylvania P, 1997, 151-167.

Keesey, Pam. *Daughters of Darkness: Lesbian Vampire Tales.* San Francisco: Cleis, 1993.

Krafft-Ebing, Richard von. *Psychopathia Sexualis: A Medico-Forensic Study.* New York: Login, 1908.

Kristeva, Julia. *An Essay on Abjection.* Trans. Leon S. Roudiez. New York: Columbia UP, 1982.

Lawrence, D. H. *The Rainbow.* Hamburg: Albatross Verlag G.M.B.H., 1936.

Lee, Hyun-Jung. "'One for Ever': Desire, Subjectivity and the Threat of the Abject in Sheridan Le Fanu's Carmilla." *Vampires: Myths and Metaphors of Enduring Evil.* Ed. Peter Day. Amsterdam: Rodopi, 2006. 21-38.

Ledger, Sally. *The New Woman: Fiction and Feminism at the Fin de Siècle.* Manchester: Manchester UP, 1997.

McDonald, Beth E. *The Vampire as Numinous Experience: Spiritual Journeys with the Undead in British and American Literature.* Jefferson, NC: McFarland, 2004.

Nead, Lynda. *Myths of Sexuality: Representations of Women in Victorian Britain.* Oxford: Blackwell, 1990.

O'Malley, Patrick. *Catholicism, Sexual Deviance, and Victorian Gothic Culture.* Cambridge: Cambridge UP, 2006.

Oosterhuis, Harry. "Reinheit und Verfolgung." *Österreichische Zeitschrift für Geschichtswissenschaften* 3 (1994): 388-409.

Palmer, Paulina. *Lesbian Gothic Transgressive Fictions.* London: Cassell, 1999.

Parker, Christopher. *Gender Roles and Sexuality in Victorian Literature.* Aldershot: Scolar, 1995.

Patterson, Kathy Davis. "'Haunting Back': Vampire Subjectivity in The Gilda Stories." *Femspec* 6.1 (2005): 35-57.

Pharr, Mary: "Vampiric Appetite in *I Am Legend, 'Salem's Lot,* and *The Hunger.*" *The Blood Is the Life: Vampires in Literature.* Ed. Leonard G. Heldreth and Mary Pharr. Ohio: Bowling Green U Popular P, 1999. 93-103.

Polidori, John. "The Vampyre." *The Penguin Book of Vampire Stories.* Ed. Alan Ryan. New York: Penguin, 1988. 7-24.

"Queer." *The Concise Oxford English Dictionary.* 11th ed. 2004, 1177.

----, *The Oxford Dictionary of English Etymology.* 7th ed. 1979, 731.

Radicalesbians. "The Woman Identified Woman." The Second Wave: A Reader in Feminist Theory. Ed. Linda Nicholson. London: Routledge, 1997. 153-157.

Rich, Adrienne. "Compulsory Heterosexuality and Lesbian Existence." *Signs* 5.4 (Summer 1980): 631-660.

Rymer, James Malcolm. "Varney the Vampyre, or, the Feast of Blood." *The Penguin Book of Vampire Stories.* Ed. Alan Ryan. New York: Penguin, 1988. 26-35.

Scott, Jody. *I, Vampire.* New York: The Women's Press Liminted, 1986.

Senf, Carol A. "Daughters of Lilith: Women Vampires in Popular Culture." *The Blood Is the Life: Vampires in Literature.* Ed. Leonard G. Heldreth and Mary Pharr. Ohio: Bowling Green U Popular P, 1999. 199-216.

Signorotti, Elizabeth. "Repossessing the Body: Transgressive Desire in 'Carmilla' and *Dracula.*" Criticism 38, 4 (1996): 607-632.

Stoker, Bram. *Dracula.* 1897. Penguin Popular Classics Edition. London: Penguin, 1994.

Waltje, Jörg. *Blood Obsession: Vampires, Serial Murder, and the Popular Imagination.* New York: Lang, 2005.

Willis, Martin. "Le Fanu's 'Carmilla', Ireland, and Diseased Vision." *Literature and Science.* Ed. Sharon Ruston. Cambridge: Brewer, 2008. 111-129.

Wittig, Monique. *The Straight Mind and Other Essays.* Boston: Beacon Press, 2002.

Zedler, Johann Heinrich. *Großes vollständiges Universal-Lexikon.* 2nd ed. Graz: Akad. Druck- u. Verl.-Anst., 1997. 328-335.

INDEX

Printed in the USA
CPSIA information can be obtained
at www.ICGtesting.com
LVHW040950270923
759489LV00005B/37